Anonymous

Another Sketch of the Reign of George III

From the Year 1780 to 1790

Anonymous

Another Sketch of the Reign of George III
From the Year 1780 to 1790

ISBN/EAN: 9783337096175

Printed in Europe, USA, Canada, Australia, Japan

Cover: Foto ©ninafisch / pixelio.de

More available books at **www.hansebooks.com**

A SKETCH

OF THE

REIGN

OF

GEORGE THE THIRD.

A SKETCH

OF THE

REIGN

OF

GEORGE THE THIRD,

FROM

1780,

TO THE CLOSE OF THE YEAR

1790.

LONDON:
PRINTED FOR J. DEBRETT,
OPPOSITE BURLINGTON HOUSE, PICCADILLY,
M DCC XCI.

A

SKETCH, &c. &c.

TO those who open the volume of history with a view to improve their understanding; who are competent to carry their researches beyond the external appearance of events, and to speculate on the concealed causes which produce the elevation, or accelerate the decline of empires, there is not, perhaps, in the annals of time a period more pregnant with political matter, than the one which has elapsed between the year 1780 and the present time. In that short interval, we have seen the British Empire, which had embraced both hemispheres, and to which India and America were only provinces:

vinces; which had successfully opposed, under the auspices of the late Earl of Chatham, the combined force of the House of Bourbon, and, after giving laws to Europe, had dispensed peace to mankind: we have seen this empire shaken to its basis, convulsed at home, and assailed on every side; vainly invoking the aid of that perfidious Princess, whose fleets we had conducted into seas unknown to her barbarous subjects, and whose victorious banner we had taught to fly on the shore of Greece and of Asia Minor. It was from her ungrateful hand that England, already bending beneath the complicated calamities of domestic division and of foreign war, was destined to receive the final blow, which unnerved our arm, and compelled us, reluctantly, to assemble our distant legions for the protection of the capital, and the preservation of our existence. It is unnecessary to say, that I allude to the " Armed Neutrality;" a measure which originated from the cabinet of Catherine the Second, although it was followed

followed by all the Baltic Powers; and the retribution due to which, however long delayed, is now probably near its accomplishment. But we have not only seen the British monarchy, in common with other states and kingdoms, oppressed by enemies, and sinking under the weight of adverse fortune, or pusillanimous and feeble counsels: we have seen this expiring and diminished empire (unlike to every other, and in this dissimilarity laying the strongest claim to the admiration of mankind), within the transitory period of only ten years, rise from a state of humiliation and depression, readjust her scattered insignia, resume her ancient lustre, and wing a sublimer flight than she had ever held across the political expanse. It is in vain that the most laborious research would endeavour to parallel this extraordinary renovation in the history of modern Europe. It is only in the Athenian or Roman Annals; it is only at the fatal periods of Marathon, and of Cannæ, that we see any example of a republic suddenly and rapidly emerging from the lowest point of ruin and calamity, into greater power and grandeur than she had previously enjoyed.

The Austrian Eagle, which, under Charles the Fifth and Ferdinand the Second, had soared so high, and which had even nearly extinguished all the Germanic liberties; stripped of its plumage by Gustavus Adolphus, and chained to the earth by the manacles which were imposed on it at the Treaty of Westphalia, long slumbered in peaceful bondage, 'till Marlborough released the Imperial captive, and, once again restored it to freedom, though not to its former greatness.

Spain, which under Philip the Second had menaced Europe, and seemed almost in possession of her inordinate projects of ambition; which fitted out her invincible Armada for the subjection of England, while she prepared to place an Infanta on the throne of France: Exhausted by her own perpetual efforts, and having drained the treasures of the new world, in vainly attempting to reduce a revolted province, funk at once into impotent infignificance; and now, after the lapfe of two hundred years, appears to be only flowly emerging from poverty and weaknefs.

Sweden, which like a torrent overran Poland, Saxony, and Denmark, at the commencement of the prefent century; and which, conducted by the frantic valour of Charles the Twelfth, appeared ready to plant her triumphant ftandards on the walls of Mofcow, was hurled in a fingle day from the zenith of power and glory. All her laurels withered at Pultowa; and fince that memorable æra, her melancholy and fteril annals contain nothing which can awaken curiofity, or intereft mankind, though more than feventy years have elapfed fince Charles expiated his wild and deftructive projects of ambition under the walls of Frederickfhall. At the moment when I am writing, a Prince, emulous of the fame of Guftavus Adolphus, and adorned with qualities which, in a more fortunate period, might have

have restored the drooping genius of Sweden, and re-instated her in those provinces which she has lost, is endeavouring to supply the inherent deficiencies arising from the impoverished and depopulated state of his dominions, by personal fortitude and ability. He has even made an effort not inglorious, to check the Russian progress, and to assert the ancient pre-eminence of his sceptre in the Baltic. These, however, are feeble attempts, and serve rather to remind us of what Sweden once was, than to awaken any well-grounded expectation that she can again resume her former situation in Europe.

Even France, the favoured country of nature; blessed with a happy diversity of climates; enriched with the choicest and most delicate productions of a luxuriant soil; embracing the Atlantic and the Mediteranean seas; formed for empire, for dominion, and for superiority among the European kingdoms; uniting in herself every natural advantage which industry can bestow, or commerce can procure;
inured

inured to habits of obedience and loyalty, as well as trained to conqueſt and to war: France herſelf, after the ſevere chaſtiſement which Louis the Fourteenth, towards the concluſion of his reign, received from Eugene and Marlborough, remained almoſt ſupine and torpid during thirty years which ſucceeded the Treaty of Utrecht; content to cultivate the peaceful olive, and oppreſſed under the load of public debt, which the inſatiable and ruinous ambition of her ſovereign had incurred. It was not 'till Marechal Saxe awoke her dormant genius, and revived in his perſon the ſublime talents which have equalled him with Condè and Turenne, that France, in any meaſure, reſumed her aſcendant, or ſeemed again to occupy her natural pre-eminence among the ſtates of Europe.

It cannot be more curious to enquire, than it muſt be inſtructive to aſcertain, whence has ariſen this characteriſtic, and peculiar principal of reſuſcitation, if I may be allowed the expreſſion, which, in a ſhort a short space of time, has raised England from her depression; and has enabled her, unlike the other surrounding monarchies, to profit of her very misfortunes, and to engraft splendor and power upon her losses and defeats.

Where are we to search for this vivifying source of renovation? Is it in her spirit of commercial enterprize; in her undiminished industry; in her numerous and ingenious manufactures, which have penetrated into almost every province of the civilized world? Doubtless, these causes have contributed much to extricate and to restore the nation; but, efficacious and salutary as their tendency and operation are, they cannot be considered as adequate to so great a work.

It was requisite that Providence should extend its tutelary care, to prolong the life and reign of a Prince, inexpressibly dear and necessary to his people; whose experience, matured by years and chastened by adversity, might, and could alone be equal to the arduous task of selecting from
among

among his subjects, those who from capacity and virtue were competent to heal the wounds, and restore the energy of the commonwealth. It was requisite that a minister should arise, who, to incorruptible integrity, and unblemished manners, should unite strength of mind, severe œconomy, vigilance which never sleeps, eloquence to captivate, and vigour to subdue. Rare, and almost unexampled combination of endowments, conferred by Heaven on those, and on those only, whom, in her wise dispensations, she destines to sustain, and restore a sinking monarchy! Yet such a minister, may it be asserted without flattery, has this age and country seen: Such an administration have we already enjoyed during near seven years; and to it may be justly ascribed those auspicious and happy events, which the present age regards with mingled wonder and admiration, and which will be long commemorated by a grateful posterity.

To trace the gradual progression from the darkness of 1780, to the bright sunshine

shine of the present moment: to pourtray some of the leading characters and events, which have successively marked and distinguished the intermediate time: to describe that stormy and tempestuous period, which, during two years, shook the cabinet, the palace, and the throne, till in 1784, the present minister, after a long and painful struggle, advanced into open day, and commenced his brilliant career: to mark the principal and most discriminating features of his domestic government, and foreign policy: to take a general and rapid survey of the causes which have involved the monarchy of France in anarchy, and which seem to threaten that beautiful portion of Europe with all the horrors of civil war, of bloodshed, and of bankruptcy: finally, to deduce this interesting series of events from the period at which I have commenced, to the time when I shall lay before the public the picture which I am now designing: these are the objects of the present attempt. I am sensible of all its difficulty and delicacy.

cacy. I know how dangerous it is to hold up even truths to the eye of prejudice, or of party; and how reluctantly we allow the veil to be withdrawn from before the political sanctuary, when we are interested in its concealment or its defence. I feel how invidious is the task of appreciating the motives and actions of our cotemporaries, our friends, and our fellow citizens. I am not insensible, above all, of my own incapacity to treat of matters yet recent; and obscured by the passions and interests of the great actors themselves. But, great as these impediments are, they cannot induce me to relinquish my design. What narrative can be so instructive, or so interesting *to* the present age, as the history *of* the present age? " Veteris populi " Romani, prospera, vel adversa, claris " scriptoribus memorata sunt:" Of the last ten years, no sketch has yet been offered to the public. It will be my province, " sine ira et studio, quorum causas procul " habeo;" with as much impartiality as the subject itself, and the infirmities of our nature will admit, to delineate the events which have paſſed in ſucceſſion be-before us, ſince the diſaſtrous period where the preſent memoirs commence.

The Britiſh empire, which only a few years preceding that æra had appeared to be ſo elevated and durable, then exhibited a melancholy and inſtructive leſſon of the mutability of human greatneſs. Civil war, which had commenced its deſtruction, was aided by a combination of the firſt European powers to compleat its fall. Her fleets and armies, accuſtomed to conqueſt, retreated before the navies of France and Spain. Her ſhores, ſo long unuſed to hoſtile invaſion, were threatened and inſulted. Her finances groaning beneath new and annual loans, conducted upon injudicious or ruinous principles, ſeemed to approach that point, beyond which public credit cannot exiſt or ſurvive. Diſcord raiſed her flaming brand in the capital, the ſenate, and the cabinet. London, ſcarcely eſcaped from conflagration and pillage, looked forward to a general ſuſpenſion of commerce,

merce, and to national infolvency, as imminent and almoft inevitable. Clamour and difcontent filled the kingdom, and characterifed the affemblies of the people in the different counties. Ireland, difdaining all further appeal except to the fword, and treading in the traces of America, armed her fubjects, not fo much for defence and protection, as for the purpofes of emancipation from the yoke of England. In the Britifh Channel, once facred from foreign intrufion, the iflands of Jerfey were repeatedly attacked. Spain, which had already re-united Minorca to her crown, held Gibraltar befieged, and meditated the conqueft of the Floridas. Every month brought accounts of the diminution of the Weft India Iflands, which fucceffively fell into the hands of France; while Jamaica, left almoft to her own internal capacities of defence, expected with trembling folicitude the long meditated invafion by the united fleets of the Houfe of Bourbon.

In India, Hyder Ally, the fcourge of the

the British nation, aided by the arms of France, was on the point of exterminating and expelling us from our moſt ancient poſſeſſions. Madras was menaced by famine, as well as by war; while Bengal itſelf ſcarcely ſuſtained the preſſure of the Mahrattas; and the vaſt fabric which Clive had cemented with a profuſion of European and Aſiatic blood, was ready to crumble with as much rapidity as it had been originally conſtructed.

In America, the names of Clinton and Cornwallis had ſucceeded to thoſe of Howe. New armies had occupied the poſts of their victorious, but departed predeceſſors. The war which had long blazed in the midland provinces, was then principally transferred to thoſe of Carolina and Virginia. Uſeleſs trophies and barren laurels appeared to be the only advantages, which we were deſtined to derive or acquire. Impenetrable woods and impaſſible moraſſes, in the centre of which freedom had diſplayed her banner, perpetually baffled all the exertions of valour,

lour, military skill, and perseverance, England began to awake from her dream of subjugating the Thirteen Colonies, and already meditated the dereliction of that ruinous and expensive undertaking; while her pride, her honour, and her indignation still propelled her forward, and amused her with hopes of success, which constantly vanished at a nearer view. Like the Roman empire under Gallienus, that of Britain seemed to approach the period of all its glories, and to be menaced with impending and total subversion.

From this gloomy and dejecting picture of foreign affairs, it may be judicious to pass to a more animated, if not a more exhilerating scene; that which was exhibited at home in the two houses of Parliament. The principal figure which here presented itself, was the first minister, Lord North, struggling against a host of enemies, and slowly retreating before them, while they pressed forward with loud and repeated clamours. A thousand javelins hung upon his

his political buckler, the points of which were continually broken and turned aside by his urbanity, his ready and pleasant wit, or his able and ingenious reasonings, when sufficiently stung by the reproaches which were heaped on him, to awaken and to rouse his torpid parts. Inur'd to the habits of parliamentary debate, master of all the science of ministerial evasion or defence: though destitute of energy and coercion of character, yet eloquent, mild, persuasive, and blessed with an almost insuperable tranquillity of temper, he patiently saw the storm exhaust itself; and looked round, serene and placid, to that powerful phalanx, which, long accustomed to obey, still closely adhered to him under every circumstance of public distress, and never abandoned him in the hour of necessity. Even the lethargic and soporific qualities of his body, as they frequently prevented him from either hearing or feeling the invectives of opposition, in some measure disarmed and blunted their edge; while slumbers, which so often fly the couch of princes, not unusually visited Lord North amidst all the din and tumult of the Treasury Bench. Near him sat the American Secretary, Lord George Germain; whose more irritable nerves, and more communicative or unguarded character, afforded materials and scope for continual attack. Gifted with extraordinary natural endowments, though little cultivated by polite letters, or adorned by science; active, persevering, decisive, and capable of conducting the greatest affairs of state, he was yet pursued by the same fatality which had blasted his early prospects of greatness. Unsuccessful in age upon the plains of America, as he had been unfortunate in youth upon those of Germany, he vainly invoked an exhausted nation, and a discontented Parliament, to continue a war, which, however just and necessary in its origin, had become odious and ungrateful, from a long series of ill success. Loyal to his Sovereign, pertinacious in his favourite measure of subjecting America,

D and

and conceiving his own political situation inseparably connected with the final success of that attempt, he adhered inflexibly to it, and regarded its prosecution as a sacred principle, from which no obstacles could induce him to recede.

Mr. Ellis, who for near half a century, since the times of Walpole and Pelham, had occupied a place under Government, continued to retain his ancient corner on the Treasury Bench; while Mr. Dundas, whose pliant and versatile talents have adapted themselves to almost every Administration, and whose abilities are calculated to strengthen and support any, was seated nearer to the centre of action, and boldly presented himself at the post of danger, whenever the enemy attempted to storm the outworks. His friend and companion Mr. Rigby, still enjoyed the ample revenue of the Pay Office, without a partner; and in the excesses of a voluptuous table, of wine and conviviality, drowned the recollection of tiresome debates, and more disgraceful defeats.

The

The two great luminaries of legal knowledge, Thurlow and Wedderburne, who had long occupied and adorned their seats on the same side of the house, had been successively raised to the honours of the peerage; and their empty places were filled by others far inferior in energy, dignity and capacity. Such was the aspect of ministry at the period to which I allude. On the other side of the house, Mr. Fox led on the bands of opposition in close and well conducted files, while Mr. Burke charged at the head of his irregular squadrons, and carried terror into the ranks of administration. Dunning, in defiance of nature, destitute almost of organs of articulation, monotonous and disgusting in his tones, ungraceful in his figure, possessing no external advantages, and unadorned by any factitious circumstances of birth and alliance; yet, under all these impediments, arrested the judgment, charmed the ear, and captivated the imagination, by the stream of his eloquence: though it sometimes flowed through the channels of law,

law, it was always bright, clear, and lucid. Keppel, Conway, Howe, and Barrè occupied their refpective ftations in this formidable and augmenting body, and aided the general attack upon the feeble and difmayed adherents of the minifter.

Suftain'd by the purity and integrity of his intentions; repofing on the efteem and affections of his people; and bent on the profecution of a war, which, however unfortunate in its conduct, was founded in the juft rights of his throne, no fymptom of change or alarm was to be traced in the fovereign. At no period of his reign were his fortitude and magnanimity put to fo fevere a teft, and at none were they more unfhaken. Equanimity, ferenity, and dignity appeared in his features, and pervaded his manners, even in moments of the moft acute perfonal fuffering. That piety, and that refignation to the difpenfations of Providence, which has always formed fo diftinguifhing a part of his character, eminently gilded the gloom of this melancholy portion of his reign, preceded and

and followed by scenes of prosperity and glory. Such was the sublime and affecting spectacle which George the Third exhibited to mankind, amidst the convulsions of every kind which menaced his domestic tranquillity, diminished his empire, and attacked him with augmenting violence.

To the limited and erring eye of man, incapable of pervading futurity, and of removing the darkness which surrounds it, Louis the Sixteenth then presented a very different and a much more enviable figure. Fortunate in having succeeded to a prince, who was sunk in dissolute pleasures, and lost to all public exertion before his reign expired, he ascended the throne of Henry the Fourth, under every flattering circumstance of youth and of prosperity. His want of any eminent talents seemed to be amply compensated by œconomy, application, decorum of manners, and, above all, by a selection of wise and able ministers. A successful war, which eclipsed and obliterated the disgraces and defeats, sustained

tained by France in her laſt rupture with England, endeared him to a loyal and affectionate nation, characteriſed for ages by its predilection and attachment to its monarchs. A Queen, diſtinguiſhed by endowments of mind, of manners, and of perſon, not leſs than by her high rank and imperial deſcent, had formed the bond of connexion between the Houſes of Bourbon and of Auſtria, while ſhe rendered Verſailles the reſidence of pleaſure, gaiety, and magnificence. France appeared to re-aſcend in the ſcale of Europe, in the ſame proportion as Great Britain declined; and flattery, if not reaſon, already predicted the revival of the proud age of Lewis the Fourteenth. But, to confound the ſpeculations of policy, and to evince the haſty tranſitions of human greatneſs, it was preciſely at this very juncture that the ſeeds were ſown, which we have ſince ſeen matured; which have already overturned the very elements of order and government, ſtained the palace of Verſailles with blood, and menace the extinction of property,

property, perſonal ſecurity, and every thing dear to mankind. The troops who were ſent as auxiliaries to the rebellious provinces of Great Britain beyond the Atlantic, ſpeedily imbibed that ſpirit of freedom, which they were commanded to defend; and did not relinquiſh theſe ſentiments ſo incompatible with abſolute monarchy, when they returned to their native country. On the other hand, the anticipation of the public revenue, which was neceſſarily produced by a war, however glorious and ſuccefsful, added to the immoderate expences of a diſſipated and luxurious court, ſoon reduced the King to adopt a meaſure, which though diſintereſted and even patriotic, opened the way to ſhake his throne. Louis the Sixteenth was perſuaded to break the royal houſehold, to diſmifs about four hundred officers holding poſts immediately about his perſon, and to content himſelf with a leſs expenſive and ſplendid eſtabliſhment. Perhaps no advice more replete with calamity, could have been conceived or followed.

lowed. The pomp and external paraphernalia of majesty being once withdrawn; and the numbers of nobility attached to the sovereign by interest, vanity, or affection, being once disbanded, the throne was left naked, unprotected, and exposed to insult. Experience has evinced its destructive tendency; and has shewn that only a limited monarch, who reigns in the affections of his subjects, and whose interests are intimately blended with those of his people, can remain an object of respect and homage, divested of the splendor and protection of a royal court, and numerous household.

The Empress Queen, Maria Theresa, closed at this period a reign of forty years, marked by the most striking vicissitudes of prosperous and of adverse fortune. During the existence of the powerful combination which shook her throne in the commencement of her life, she exhibited the most undaunted magnanimity, the greatest resources of mind, and a courage superior to her sex. Driven from Vienna in 1741, while

while Bohemia and Auſtria were over-run by the French and Bavarians, ſhe found protection and ſuccours in the loyalty of her Hungarian ſubjects, who at ſight of her beauty, youth, and misfortunes, forgot their hereditary enmity and jealouſy of the Imperial houſe from which ſhe ſprung. The afternoon and evening of her reign, though frequently diſturbed by foreign wars, were paſſed by her in the diſcharge of every duty due from a ſovereign to her people. Mild, clement, humane, munificent, and ever extending the proofs of her parental tenderneſs to her wide extended dominions, ſhe was idolized by the Hungarians, beloved by the Flemings, and dear to every order of citizens. That piety and fortitude which had characterized her life, accompanied and brightened her dying moments. Her crowns deſcended to her ſon Joſeph; a Prince who had given premature expectations of genius and capacity, and whoſe emulation of the King of Pruſſia promiſed to render him worthy of ſo great an antagoniſt. But Europe was soon undeceived in this favorable anticipation of the talents of Joseph the Second. Agitated with perpetual and varying schemes of conquest: restless, and incapable of repose: planning innovations in religion, in manners, and in civil life, which were no sooner executed than revoked: oppressive and despotic, without the art either of concealing these qualities, or of rendering their effects palatable to his subjects: menacing at the same moment the just franchises of the Netherlands, and the antient liberties of Hungary: dreaded in the empire, and detested in his own capital: anxious to enlarge the limits of his dominions, even at the expence of faith and justice: rapacious of ecclesiastical property, and profuse only of the blood of his people; Joseph soon alienated the affections of every rank, and closed a tempestuous reign, unregretted, and unlamented; leaving the House of Austria in embarrassments, produced by his violence and ambition, scarcely inferior to those which had so nearly overturned and extinguished it, it, at the death of his grandfather Charles the Sixth.

Two illustrious and extraordinary Princes then filled the thrones of Muscovy and of Prussia. A woman was still destined to sway the sceptre of the Czars, and to govern the immense regions extending from the Frozen to the Caspian Sea. Unequalled in magnificence, and unconquerable in war, Catherine the Second had enlarged the limits of her vast dominions, covered the Black Sea with Russian fleets, and threatened the entire subversion of the Ottoman power. Protectress of the sciences and liberal arts, she cultivated the friendship of d'Alembert, courted the correspondence and the praises of Voltaire, and, like Louis XIV., extended her munificence to men of letters throughout every kingdom of Europe. Intoxicated with success, and elevated to the summit of human grandeur and felicity, she forgot the friendly hand which had aided her arms, and taught them the way to victory; while dreaded and admired in every quarter

ter of the globe, she seemed to have chained the inconstancy of fortune, and to defy the changes and clouds which so frequently darken the conclusion of a female reign.

Frederic, covered with laurels, and retired from Berlin to the solitary magnificence of Potzdam; in the bosom of literary repose, and sinking under the pressure of augmenting infirmities, advanced towards the termination of his memorable life and reign. Alienated from, or indifferent to the misfortunes of England, he regarded with a philosophic and averted eye her present unequal contest against so many powers; and extended no relief, nor made any exertion in favour of his antient ally.

Portugal alone, among so many neutral, or hostile states, ventured at this distressful moment, to give some affirmative marks of friendship to the crown of Great Britain.

While Europe exhibited this aspect, so little calculated to awaken hope, fresh losses

losses and defeats awaited the arms of England beyond the Atlantic. The capture of the Island of St. Eustatius, which, on its first promulgation, had diffused a general joy throughout the nation, produced in the event only obloquy to the captors, and a suspension the most untimely and injurious in our naval and military exertions; while the troops, which should have acted with vigour against the enemy, were sunk in inactivity, or occupied in plunder.

As the year advanced, new islands were lost, and new disgraces incurred; 'till the climax of national calamity attained its ultimate point, by the surrender of an army of seven thousand men, who laid down their arms before Washington and Rochambeau, on the shore of the Chesapeake. After six years of mutual slaughter and alternate success, the genius of America triumphed, and this last unexampled victory for ever confirmed her independence. The intelligence, when it was received in England, shook the already tottering Administration, and precipitated its fall.

Dismay,

Dismay and terror pervaded the cabinet, and agitated the counsels. The Opposition, conscious of the augmenting distress and fluctuating irresolution of the first minister, called aloud for an explicit avowal of his renunciation of any further efforts to subjugate the revolted colonies. The expressive silence of Lord North to these peremptory demands, left no room to doubt either of his sentiments or his wishes; and the Secretary for America, retiring from a situation no longer tenable, after a rude attack from Lord Carmarthen, was received into the quiet bosom of the House of Lords. The enemy rushed into the breach which this disunion had occasioned, and already beheld the prize within their grasp. The Administration, however, still lingered, though destitute of animation or energy; a feeble and ineffectual effort was even made to prolong their existence, by the substitution of Mr. Ellis in the place of Lord George Germain; but this step served only to accelerate their dissolution. Opposition, eager to seize the prey, and ac-
quiring

quiring force as they advanced, pushed on towards the citadel; 'till Lord North, on the 20th of March, 1782, exhibited the singular and humiliating spectacle of a First Minister divesting himself of all the insignia of office, before a crowded House of Commons; and announcing his resignation to an astonished audience, who scarcely credited the fact of which they were witnesses. The novelty and effect of this extraordinary surrender of power, were encreased by its being equally sudden and unexpected. Neither his friends nor his enemies were aware of the blow; and even his sovereign did not suspect, 'till almost the very instant in which he executed his purpose, that any such was meditated or intended. It is nugatory and unnecessary here to enquire, whether it was principally produced by timidity, fatigue, or disgust. Probably, by a combination of all these emotions; and unquestionably by a very unforeseen and hasty determination.

In this disarmed and unprepared situation, without either time or ability for
framing

framing a new miniftry, the King could only furrender at difcretion. He did fo; and the royal garrifon, entered by ftorm, was plundered by the conquerors. Three garters were found among the fpoils, and which ferved to decorate the principal chieftains. Offices and pofts were diftributed at their arbitrary pleafure; and a new Adminiftration foon appeared, compofed of motley materials, and evincing in its very formation and component parts, the principles of fpeedy diffolution. The feeble genius of Lord Rockingham prefided over it, but could infpire no heat or energy into the heterogeneous mafs. Ill calculated for fo arduous and delicate a ftation, he wanted talents to guide, and animate the complicated machine of which he was only the oftenfible leader. Mr. Fox and the Earl of Shelburne occupied the two Secretaryfhips of State; while Keppel, raifed to the peerage for his fervices on the 27th of July, 1778, fucceeded to the prefidency of the vacant Board of Admiralty.

It is not my intention minutely to delineate

neate or depicture the measures of this transitory Administration, just shewn to the British, as Marcellus was to the Roman people; and snatched away by an extinction as hasty, but not as much lamented. I have ever regarded the short period of its duration, as the last and lowest point of national and royal depression. Though illuminated by a victory, which has shed an unexampled lustre over the annals of England, no ray of it reflected upon the Ministry: they had vilified and persecuted the great naval commander who obtained it, previous to his departure for his station: they recalled him in the very moment of his conquests. The annals of that period, circumscribed within three months, are marked by the humiliating and fruitless attempts of the Government to obtain peace from Holland; though illusory promises and assurances of success had been held out to parliament, and to the country, by Mr. Fox, before his entry upon office. The peerage, in the almost only instance where it was conferred, was

F extorted

extorted from the sovereign, without even the decencies of respect, or of request; and the extraordinary spectacle of a newly-created Peer kissing the King's hand in the Queen's drawing room, in violation of all form or usage, was reserved for the Rockingham Administration to exhibit, in the person of Sir Fletcher Norton.

A bill, which without materially conducing to national œconomy, or public benefit, diminished on one hand the dignity which used to wait upon the person of the sovereign; and on the other, disarmed every succeeding minister, by leaving him scarcely any objects with which to stimulate activity, or reward merit and adherence. A bill, which by compelling every Administration, from want of offices, to multiply the peerage, as the only thing left in their power to bestow; and which, if not redressed and repealed, may eventually destroy the balance of the constitution. A bill, well known, and as

well

well characterized by the name of its eloquent, but theoretical and visionary author, was introduced, and rapidly carried through the unresisting Houses of Parliament; while the King was compelled to lend his name and aid to the completion of a law, which disbanded his houshold, and disarmed his authority.

This unwise and impolitic attack upon the majesty of the throne, was properly accompanied and succeeded by similar invasions of the hereditary franchises of the people. Under the specious allegation of extinguishing the corrupt influence of the Crown, a great and industrious body of men, the officers of the customs, were deprived of their just and unalienable right to vote in elections for their representatives in Parliament; and the natural reward of merit or services was converted by the Legislature, into an instrument of punishment and privation.

But, happily for the monarch and for the nation, a Ministry, in which hypocritical profession was substituted for action;

whose conquests were limited to St. James's, and whose trophies were only obtained over clerks of the Green Cloth and housekeepers, now drew near its extinction. The natural decease of the Marquis of Rockingham, which took place upon the 1st of July, 1782, can scarcely be said to have preceded, or anticipated his political dismission. He expired in the vicinity of London; regretted only by his immediate friends and adherents; esteemed as a virtuous and a well intentioned, though an inadequate Minister. His elevation to the first post in the Administration was injurious to his character as a man of talents; and he was twice destined in the present reign, to see the political fabrick which he had reared, moulder within a few months, and sink under its own pressure. Like Galba, "Major privato visus, dum privatus fuit; "et omnium consensu, capax imperii, "nisi imperasset."

Released by this interposition of fortune, from a bondage equally severe and humiliating,

humiliating, the Sovereign made a felection from among his fervants, more confonant to his own perfonal inclinations, as well as more calculated to advance the public fervice. The Earl of Shelburne affumed the vacant Treafurer's ftaff, which had dropped from the hand of the deceafed Marquis; while the honeft and virtuous incapacity of the late Chancellor of the Exchequer, was fupplied by equal probity and integrity, but accompanied with thofe fublime and early talents, which Mr. Pitt alone has difplayed and fuftained in the prefent age. Having declined the proffered advances of the late Miniftry, and having refufed to form any inferior part of, or accept any fecondary fituation under that fyftem, he now firft appeared in the front ranks of government; and evinced to an aftonifhed nation, that in a poft fo arduous as that of the fuperintendance of the complicated finances of an exhaufted and impoverifhed country, he could unite the energy and vigour of youth, with the

maturity

maturity and experience of more advanced life.

Some subordinate alterations in other departments of state completed the new Administration; which, at its commencement was favoured by the advanced period of the year and session, and the prorogation of Parliament which naturally followed. The adherents of Lord Rockingham filled the Lower House with loud clamours and pointed insinuations, against the supposed motives and authors of a change so inimical, as they asserted, to the best interests of the monarchy. Mr. Fox in a manly and magnanimous, Mr. Burke, in a querulous and reluctant manner, respectively resigned their situations. The impassioned exclamations of the latter were only interrupted and extinguished by the arrival of the Black Rod, and the summons to attend the Chancellor at the bar of the House of Lords. The session closed; and oblivion already drew her veil across the departed Administration, while new convulsions, and new scenes of political confusion

confusion were silently, but rapidly, generating in the womb of time.

Peace, which for so many years had fled, now prepared to return. Inactivity, and a premature suspension of hostility beyond the Atlantic, gradually opened the passage to universal tranquillity in Europe. America, already declared independent by the Legislature, no longer occupied the arms or efforts of Great Britain. Holland, divided by the Orange and the Republican factions, feebly sustained her portion of the common attack. France, arrested in the midst of all her conquests by the arm of Rodney, saw her boasted navy scattered over the Western world; happy to escape the pursuit of a victorious fleet, and to sink undisturbed, in the havens of Martinico, or of Boston. It only remained to humble the arrogance of Spain; who, insolent with unaccustomed success, and elated with the trophies acquired at Minorca, and in Florida, had assembled her forces of every kind round the rock of Gibraltar, and already anticipated the reunion

union of that proud fortress to her dominions. To indulge at once the gratification of national vanity, as well as the acquisition of glory, a Prince of the Blood Royal of France was invited to quit the effeminate pleasures of Versailles, and to become a spectator of its reduction from the Spanish camp. Preparations only inferior to those of Philip the Second against Elizabeth, were made to accelerate and secure so favourite an object of the court of Madrid; while all Europe might be said, in common with the Count d'Artois, to have fixed their eyes upon this animating spectacle. I need not relate the event; inscribed in characters which must last as long as military fame and valour are revered among men. The formidable armaments of Charles the Third perished under the superior fire of the garrison; and the miserable victims who escaped from the conflagration, were indebted for their lives to the exertions of that very enemy, for whose destruction they had been assembled.

Under

Under this singular blaze of glory and success was terminated a war, which had been marked during its progress with every circumstance adverse to England, and which, at many periods, had menaced its very existence. Negociations, prolonged throughout the autumn, produced a general pacification at the beginning of 1783; the terms of which, however widely different they were from those which Great Britain dictated at the treaties of Utrecht and of Fontainbleau, seemed neither ignominious nor disadvantageous, in the enfeebled state of the finances and resources of the country. France restored almost all her acquisitions, while Spain retained her conquests; and Holland, which had tardily and reluctantly been forced from her pacific system, was abandoned by her allies, and left to expiate by concessions, the departure from her ancient policy and connexions.

But the waves of party, which had been so long and so violently agitated, could not immediately subside with the extinction

extinction of hostilities. The two powerful factions, who had successively possessed, and been deprived of the government, however adverse they were to each other, yet united in their common opposition to the new intruders. The character of the First Lord of the Treasury, though distinguished by many imposing qualities of mind, by ingratiating and popular manners, and by an enlarged acquaintance with the foreign interests of England; yet wanted that stamp of probity and principle, without which a great nation never confers esteem and confidence. Insincerity and duplicity were ascribed to him by his enemies. Accusations and suspicions were circulated, possibly originating only in calumny, which arraigned his purity of conduct as a Minister, and insinuated his acquisition of personal wealth by the abuse of his high situation, during the progress of the late negociations, to the sordid purposes of private gain. Doubts of this complexion, however unauthenticated or unjust they may be supposed, yet,

by

by operating on the public, equally indifposed them towards the peace, and towards its author.

To these obvious and ostensible causes of his dismission, may be added the extraordinary and almost inexplicable indifference which marked his conduct, towards preserving a situation, which it had been the leading and predominant object of his life to acquire. Parliament met, and after long and violent debates, renewed at various times, expressed its disapprobation of the peace recently concluded, though by a very small majority. It is even highly probable that this mark of their dissatisfaction would not have been attended or followed by any such affirmative proofs of national resentment, as to have compelled a Minister of firmness and rectitude to retire from his public situation. Whether any consciousness of a deficiency in either of these qualities, or whether motives more concealed and unascertainable actuated the Earl of Shelburne; it is certain that he did not hesitate to take the warning which

which had been given him, and to lay down his office without delay.

But though he had embraced this pufillanimous and precipitate part, the Chancellor of the Exchequer, animated by feelings of integrity, loyalty, and duty to his Prince and to his country, generoufly refufed to abandon them to the refentments and difcretionary mandates of two factions, who had agreed to a mutual facrifice of principle, and even of decency, in order to gratify their thirft of power. After a manly and magnanimous, but ineffectual ftruggle, he was however compelled to yield to fo unequal a force. The Sovereign, who had vainly endeavoured to compofe a new Adminiftration, and who had been befieged in his own palace during fix weeks, found the lines of circumvallation too ftrong to force, and furrendered a fecond time prifoner of war. The two victorious chieftains, who had agreed to bury all paft caufes of refentment in oblivion, entered the breach in triumph, bound their captive, pofted their centinels, and invefted themfelves in the spoils which their conduct had acquired. The larger share however of these emoluments fell to Mr. Fox; and the Treasury was transferred from the mild incapacity of Lord Rockingham, whom death had removed, to the laborious, but limited and subservient talents of the Duke of Portland. Lord North, who did not feel with Cæsar, that " the first situation " in a village out-valued the second in an " empire ", was content with the inferior portion of power and profit, allotted him by the liberality of his new associates, and mixed in the cavalcade, which he had so long conducted. Too happy to obtain an amnesty for the misfortunes of his Administration, and soothed with the unaccustomed panegyrics of those who had so lately called out for axes and scaffolds; he sunk without emotion, into a subordinate office, and resigned the painful preeminence of state into hands of greater energy or ambition.

A pause succeeded to this extraordinary and eventful transfer of power; as the
monarch

monarch and the nation were equally incapable of instantly exerting any effort for their emancipation. The "Coalition" imposed their fetters upon both; and little attentive to acquire the affection, were satisfied with the submission of their prisoners. Relying on their own united strength to retain the conquests which they had made, they only began already to project the means of perpetuating and extending the term of their duration. To atchieve this object, it was indispensably necessary to reconstruct the edifice which their injudicious spirit of reform had lately overthrown; and to substitute other charges and offices in the place of those, which had been annihilated in the household of the Sovereign. These pleasing anticipations and reveries formed a grateful occupation during the recess of Parliament; and the succeeding winter was destined to see the chains, which an unprincipled ambition had fabricated, imposed with all the solemnity of legislation upon an unresisting people.

There

There is however a limit prescribed to violence, which it has ever been found impracticable to pass; and the "Coalition" was destined to be taught by it's own experience, that no combination of talents, power, or ability can sustain a Government, where all opinion of principle, or respect for character have ceased to exist, on the part of the nation towards its tyrants. Even the forms of the constitution and the sanctity of law will not prevent a generous and an enlightened country, from discerning the abuse of that authority, which while it extinguishes prerogative, militates equally against freedom. Time alone was requisite to mature these reflections; and the Administration opened the way to their own destruction, by the very means which they had concerted for placing their greatness beyond the reach of accident.

Mr. Fox introduced his celebrated "East India Bill," with all that splendor of parts, and display of ability, which has rendered him so distinguished in the history

tory of the present age. Though India was not in that department of public business, over which as Secretary of State, he personally presided, yet the superior energy of his character, and the convenient facility of his new colleague, allowed him to assume this arduous and dangerous pre-eminence. Mr. Burke's ample and inexhaustible stock of materials and documents, supplied any deficiencies of memory or local information; while the " Institutes of *Timur*," and the wisest regulations of European policy, were new-modelled by this generous legislator. The oppressions and calamities under which India had so long suffered; the peculations, committed by the servants of the Company, as well as the wanton and unprincipled wars in which they had engaged, were highly painted, and strongly reprobated. The remedy to these numerous evils was presented; and all palliatives were deprecated, as unequal to the extermination of a disease which had pervaded the whole system, which demanded a measure of more than

than ordinary vigour in the Legiflature. The Houfe of Commons yielded to thefe convincing and minifterial arguments, fo calculated to operate on their paffions as well as their judgments. The ineffectual oppofition which was made to it by Mr. Pitt, and a few perfons who adhered to him, neither retarded nor impeded the rapid progrefs of the bill. It was carried through one Houfe of Parliament by prodigious fuperiority of numbers; and it was not apprehended that the fubfervient under-derftandings of the other Houfe, generally difpofed to fee all meafures of all Adminif-trations with a favourable eye, would reject the prefent, or canvafs it with unufual feverity. The " Coalition" appeared already to touch the fhore, and to be near the accomplifhment of their moft fanguine projects of greatnefs.

The magnanimity and penetration of the Sovereign, awakened and directed by the timely exhortation of thofe who collected round the throne in this critical and dangerous conjuncture, fnatched the country from

from the impending misfortune. The great incorporated bodies in various parts of the kingdom, flowly roufed to a comprehenfion of the evil, and alarmed at the violation of the chartered rights of the firſt commercial company in the nation, appeared ready to reclaim and to defend their own threatened immunities, or properties. London led the way in thefe fymptoms of confternation, and was followed by the principal cities and provinces. Addreffes, remonftrances, and petitions, arrived from every part of Great Britain. Satire and ridicule, fo powerful in their operation upon the minds of men, united with reafon and argument to overturn a Miniftry, who had attempted to conftruct their own grandeur, equally on the ruin of the Prerogative, and the deftruction of the Conftitution. Two caricature drawings, conceived with exquifite humour, and whofe effect can perhaps be compared with nothing in our hiftory, except the fong of " Lillabullero" under James the Second, were circulated in every company. In one of thefe, the

Secretary

Secretary of State who had introduced the bill, was depictured carrying, like Atlas, the whole East-India House upon his shoulders; while the affrighted Directors, looking out of the windows, appeared vainly to invoke assistance against the violence. The other represented his triumphal entry into Dehli, the capital of his newly conquered dominions. Mr. Fox was habited in the splendid Asiatic dress of Shaw Allum; while his obedient colleague in office Lord North, degraded to the inferior nature of the trained and managed elephant, supported the victor on his back. Mr. Burke, as a trumpeter, accompanied the procession, proclaiming the virtues and trophies of this successor of Tamerlane and Aurungzebe.

The storm of national indignation, though long and tardy in forming, had now collected, and prepared to burst with the utmost violence. The House of Peers led the way, by throwing out the East-India Bill; and on the subsequent night, at a late hour, his Majesty sent to demand

H 2

mand the seals of office from the two Secretaries of State. An Administration, at the head of which was Mr. Pitt, and of which he may be said to have formed the vital principle, was instantly composed. So secure, however, were the late Ministers of their ascendancy in the House of Commons, and in such contempt were these efforts of the Crown to liberate itself held by them, that when the writ was moved for Appleby, in consequence of the new First Lord of the Treasury having vacated his seat, it was received with loud, and almost general laughter. Even those whose judgment and experience in Parliamentary matters were most respected, ventured to predict that a few weeks would see the termination of this fugitive Government, either by a gradual or a violent death. For the first time since the accession of the house of Brunswick; perhaps it may be said since the existence of the monarchy, the sovereign and the people were united in opposition to the representatives of the people. The patient and
passive

passive fortitude of Mr. Pitt sustained him, even more than his talents or integrity, during near three months that this siege continued; nor did he advise his Sovereign to have recourse to the last constitutional measure left him, that of dissolution, till above a hundred and twenty addresses, couched in terms of loyalty, and of reprobation against the attempt to overturn the prerogative, left no room to hesitate on its popularity, or on the general joy with which it would be received. The elections for the new Parliament, which at no period of the present century were ever so incorrupt, and so free from all ministerial interference, evinced beyond dispute, how odious to the nation were the principles and conduct of the late Administration. The First Minister emerged at length, from a state of the most painful exertion and depression, into political day; and the reins of Government, so long and so violently retained by the "Coalition," fell from their hands. It is from this æra that we may date the slow, but progressive elevation of the Bri-

tish

tish empire; which, shaken and convulsed during the calamitous period of the American war, had not been less agitated by internal struggles of faction, since its termination. But, before we arrive at that exhilerating scene, it may be a not less instructive, though it is a less pleasing task, to survey the picture of the empire at the moment when the present Minister commenced his Administration.

Exhausted in her finances, and deprived of vigour from the rapid succession of so many Governments, debility, languor, and decay characterised every internal department of the State. The public funds seemed to have sunk below the point of depression, to which even the misfortunes of the war had reduced them; and the confiscation which had menaced the East India Company while Mr. Fox's bill impended over their property, had operated to sink their stock below any former precedent. The revenue was diminished and invaded by the bold inroads of contraband commerce, which loudly called on the

the Legiflature for effectual interpofition and redrefs. No foreign alliance, or connexion with any of the great powers on the Continent, offered the profpect of fupport in a future war. Holland was completely governed by the Republican faction, who, under Van Berkel in the prefent, as under the De Witts in the laft century, had entered into the clofeft connexions with the Court of Verfailles; while the Prince of Orange, retaining little more than the name of Stadtholder, was reduced to a ftate of paffive infignificance. Denmark, whofe fovereigns had been connected by alliances of blood and policy with the Crown of England for near half a century; and whofe natural interefts, in oppofition to thofe of Sweden, tended to confirm thefe tyes; had departed from her ancient principles, and no longer cultivated the friendfhip of a kingdom, incapable of extending protection, or rendering itfelf refpectable in the Baltic. From the Court of Stockholm, attached for ages to France, no demonftrations of amity

amity could be expected. The Emperor, occupied in syftems of reformation, or projects of aggrandizement; planning the exchange of the Netherlands with the Elector Palatine, while he wantonly attacked the Republic of Holland, whofe troops, in defiance of the moft facred treaties, he had ejected by force from the barrier towns of Flanders: Jofeph, engaged in thefe ambitious enterprizes, and already connected with the Court of Peterfburgh, might be regarded as inimical rather than friendly to Great Britain. Ruffia continued in a ftate of fullen alienation, and Pruffia betrayed no marks of returning friendfhip; while France, ftill conducted by the fplendid and impofing counfels of Vergennes, appeared to extend, to cement, and to confirm her greatnefs.

The firft years of the prefent Adminiftration were principally characterifed by thofe beneficial regulations of commerce, and by thofe falutary meafures of finance, fo indifpenfably requifite in the fallen and impoverifhed condition of the country. An
" Eaft

"East India bill," mild and temperate in its genius, and widely different from the rapacious and arbitrary principles which had rendered the former so universally odious, was introduced, and passed into a law. The most vigorous and efficacious measures were adopted for the suppression of smuggling. The royal woods and forests, from whence so great a support to the navy ought naturally to be derived, but which had been completely abandoned, as an object of national protection, for half a century, did not escape the vigilant attention of a Minister, anxious to avail himself of every public resource. Provision was made for the slow, but certain diminution of the national debt, by the appropriation of a million sterling annually, vested in the hands of commissioners for the purchase of stock.

The consolidation of the Customs and Excise, a measure of incredible labour and detail, as well as of infinite advantage to commerce, by facilitating and simplifying the intricacies attendant on mercantile

tile transactions, and the payment of duties; a regulation which in itself might immortalize any Administration, was fully and permanently effected. It had failed under the inert and feeble efforts of Lord North; and its completion, so evidently productive of national benefit, drew applauses even from the enemies and opposers of the Minister. This long list of enlightened and patriotic measures was closed by the accomplishment of one of the greatest, but most delicate and arduous attempts, which have distinguished the present century; I mean the " Commercial Treaty with France." An enlarged and liberal policy; the greatest incitements to general industry; the extension of commerce, and the extinction of those mutual jealousies and antipathies, which have for so many ages actuated the rival monarchies of France and England: these were the characteristics and principles of a treaty, which, notwithstanding the spacious objections urged against it in Parliament, excited universal approbation, and extorted ed involuntary eulogiums. The genius of Great Britain, long obscured and fettered, began to assert its antient energy; and, liberated from domestic anarchy, prepared to re-appear on the theatre of Europe, from whence she had been banished by internal calamities and distress. The signature of the "Germanic League," at Berlin, whose object was the preservation of the liberties of the Empire against the ambition of Joseph the Second, was the first symptom exhibited of returning attention to the concerns of the Continent; and though this confederation was only acceded to by his Britannic Majesty in his capacity of Elector of Hanover, yet its effect unquestionably extended beyond its ostensible object, and recalled the English nation again to general view and consideration.

While under a wise, vigorous, and œconomical Government, we were thus resuming our ancient eminence and dignity among the European States, the clouds of discontent and civil commotion were rapidly

pidly collecting over the monarchy of France. The finances, involved since the cessation of the late war in augmenting embarrassments and inextricable difficulties, might have been found beyond the probity of a Sully, or the capacity of a Colbert, to re-establish: in the hands of Calonne, raised to the superintendance, they appeared to present a prospect of public insolvency as imminent and unavoidable. Though the Court of Versailles was much diminished in majesty and splendor by the numerous reforms which had successively taken place, yet the ministry had not substituted any judicious system of frugality, nor adopted any measures of energy and wisdom, either for the alleviation of the national burthens, and liquidation of the enormous debt contracted under the late and present King; nor (which seemed to be still more necessary for their personal safety) to guard against the gathering storm of public violence and indignation.

Louis the Sixteenth had already, in a con-

considerable degree, survived the respect, though he continued to enjoy the affection of his people. The first years of his reign, conducted by Maurepas and Vergennes, had been distinguished by the most brilliant success; which, while it dazzled and flattered the national vanity, had, in a great measure, concealed from view the ruin which it occasioned in the finances. The King possessed none of those qualities, either corporal or mental, calculated to fascinate, and to supply the place of more solid endowments. His figure was destitute of dignity, and his address awkward and embarrassed. He neither knew how to assume the open and winning manners of Henry the Fourth, nor how to adopt the majestic condescension of Louis the Fourteenth. Attached to the Queen from motives rather sensual than intellectual, and restrained by religious scruples from forming any connexions of gallantry with other women, he never, in any instance, violated his nuptial fidelity, though surrounded by courtiers anxious to anticipate, and eager

to

to administer to his desires on the first intimation. Addicted to the pleasures of the table, and sometimes induced to pass the limits of temperance and sobriety, he yielded in those moments of facility to the demands which the profusion of the Queen, and of his brother the Court d'Artois, made it necessary for them continually to renew. His own expences were moderate, and his pleasures few. The former were chiefly confined to the construction of the Castle of Compiegne, and the repairs of the palace of Versailles. The latter consisted principally in the amusement of the chace. Though much neglected in his education during the life of Louis the Fifteenth, his mind was not uninformed; and he had attained since his accession to the throne, a very considerable degree of acquaintance with polite letters, history, and geography, by his own private application and solitary study, unassisted by any aid. In the art of reigning, he had unfortunately made little progress or proficiency. Unambitious

tious and moderate in his character, he formed no views of conqueſt. He even diſapproved, though only paſſively, of the alliance with America, into which his miniſters had led him in the commencement of his reign; and ſuffered himſelf, with ſome degree of averſion and reluctance, to be made an acceſſary to the independence of the Thirteen Colonies.

His parts, however ſluggiſh, inert, and limited, yet were not inadequate to the comprehenſion and diſcharge of the high duties annexed to his ſtation. He unqueſtionably loved his people, and paſſionately deſired, at the price of every perſonal renunciation and ſacrifice, to render his reign dear to France. Averſe to cruelty, and of a nature acceſſible to the impreſſions of pity and humanity, he threw open the gates of the caſtle of Vincennes, which for ages had been one of the principal priſons of ſtate; and mitigated, in numerous inſtances, the rigour of arbitrary power, which his grandfather had ſtrengthened and abuſed.

His

His behaviour on the night of the 5th of October, 1789, has evinced, notwithstanding the doubts which have been entertained upon that point, that he did not want *personal* resolution or fortitude. But the quality in which he has been eminently deficient, and to the want of which may be principally ascribed all the late calamities of his life, is *Political* courage and decision. In times of tranquillity and repose, this defect might not have been perceived; or, if discovered, might have yet been limited in its effects: in tempestuous periods, and popular insurrections, it has convulsed the monarchy, and menaced the existence of the throne itself.

The character of the Queen, though strongly contrasted with that of Louis the Sixteenth, was perhaps still more calculated to alienate the affections and excite the clamours of the nation. Of a figure favoured by nature, and adorned by gracious and insinuating manners, she was formed to attach mankind. The short period which elapsed, subsequent to her marriage

marriage with the Dauphin, in 1770, and previous to her ascending the throne, was marked by the most general partiality, and by all the flattering prognostics of poetry and genius, who anticipated the future glories and felicity of her reign*. Her education in the court of Vienna, under the severe inspection of Maria Theresa, a Princess

* It was during this brilliant and transitory portion of her life, that she was seen by the author of a production, which has recently made its appearance in this country; and which, from the celebrity of the writer, as well as from the interest excited by the subject itself, has been read with universal avidity. It is not my intention to criticise, or to appreciate the merits of a performance, which embraces so many objects, and ranges over so vast a field, as the late Revolution in France opens to a creative imagination. With some errors and some blemishes, it appears to me to be a most extraordinary exhibition of genius, fancy, and in many parts, of deep, able, and judicious reasoning. Its author is entitled to something more than the mere approbation of every man who respects kingly power, or established Government; and who deprecates the violence of popular innovation. Perhaps the portrait of the Dauphiness may be too highly coloured; but it is the colouring of Titian, and not of a common artist. Indeed, those who remember the present Queen before the death of Louis the Fifteenth, must admit that she was then calculated to excite sentiments of personal admiration and delight, in no ordinary degree.

K   eminent

eminent for chastity and piety, seemed in some measure to guarantee the existence of these qualities in her daughter. But, Marie Antoinette appears to have inherited scarce any of the characteristic virtues or vices of the Austrian family, except her attachment to the House from whence she sprung. The fond predictions of adulation, offered to the Dauphiness, were not realized by the Queen. Her levity of manners; her expensive prodigality; her dissipations; her attachments; her retirements; perhaps, more than all these defects, her supposed abuse of the ascendant which she had acquired and preserved over her husband, gradually estranged every order of the people; and eventually, as the public embarrassments augmented, rendered her generally odious. Her actions were examined with the most severe and unjust spirit of national enquiry. Her political connections with the Imperial ambassador were as loudly arraigned on one hand, as her personal intimacy with the Comte d'Artois was strongly censured on the

the other. Imputations the moſt injurious to her fame as a woman and a wife, were ſuperadded to accuſations of her diſpoſition to ſacrifice the intereſt, and ſquander the treaſures of the kingdom over which ſhe reigned, in order to aggrandize her brother the Emperor. She was accuſed of miniſtering to the weakneſſes, and even ſtimulating the appetites of the King, with a view to avail herſelf of his fondneſs, or temporary privation of reflexion.

The continual viſits, and long interviews which ſhe accorded to Madamoiſelle Bertin, excited ſentiments of diſapprobation in thoſe, who thought the leiſure of the firſt Queen in Europe indecently thrown away in diſquiſitions upon a cap, or conſultations upon a handkerchief. Her purchaſe of the palace of St. Cloud, in the midſt of general pecuniary diſtreſs, was taxed with equal imprudence and profuſion. Her frequent retirements to Trianon were ſtigmatized, as exhibiting ſcenes unfit for the public eye. The myſterious and inexplicable tranſaction relative to the famous necklace, afferted to have been purchafed by her; although the Cardinal de Rohan and the Comteffe de la Motte were the victims of it, yet had left impreffions difadvantageous to her honour in the minds of a nation, difpofed to fee all her actions through an unfavourable medium. Her predilection for, and attachment to the Duchefs de Polignac, fuffered the moft malignant comments of fatyrical prejudice; and the liberal donations, or high employments, with which that family was diftinguifhed, neceffarily added to the load of public execration. Thefe accumulated topics of popular invective and animadverfion, were circulated with rapidity, and received with equal avidity, by an ignorant and credulous multitude, who filled the arcades of the " Palais Royal," and who imbibed the moft inveterate deteftation of their Queen, as conceiving her the author of the public diftrefs. They had already, in fome degree, marked her out as a victim to the general indignation; and anxioufly waited for the favourable occafion, occasion, which should liberate the Sovereign and the nation from the pretended evils of her influence, and leave Louis the Sixteenth to the impulse of his natural beneficence and affection for his people.

The Count de Provence, the eldest of the King's two brothers, acted a very inferior and subordinate part upon this great theatre. Either destitute of talents to excite public attention, or repressing them from motives of prudence and situation, he appeared only in the back ground; and formed a contrast to the imposing qualities which distinguished the Count d'Artois. Of a figure much more graceful and elegant than either of his brothers, this Prince was likewise adorned with more dignified, if not more courteous manners. Attached to the Queen from similarity of taste and character, he even exceeded her in profusion, expence, and dissipation. After having passed the morning on the "Plaine de Sablons," in the dress and occupations of a jockey, he only retired from these fatigues, to repose in the

palace

arms of Madamoifelle Contat. His little palace of "Bagatelle," in the "Bois de Boulogne," was at once the fcene of the moft refined and voluptuous debauch, and of the moft profligate pleafures which luxury could devife or affemble. Two fons, already advancing faft towards manhood, and whofe conftitutions feemed to promife a vigorous health, attracted the eyes of the nation, and gave him a manifeft fuperiority to the Count de Provence, whofe marriage had not been fruitful. The feeble and debilitated ftate of the Dauphin, whofe infirmities already appeared to menace a premature end, left only the Duke de Normandie between him and the eventual fucceffion to the Crown. Though not endowed with any eminent talents, yet, as being of a character more decided and affirmative than either the King or the Count de Provence, he came more forward to public view; and by his adherence to the Queen, influenced very confiderably on affairs of ftate.

At

At a greater diſtance from the throne, but decorated with the title of Firſt Prince of the Blood, was ſeen the Duke of Orleans. Poſſeſſed of an immenſe revenue, and having in reverſion all the domains of his father-in-law, the Duke de Penthievre, he might be eſteemed the richeſt ſubject in Europe. His reputation for generoſity and munificence, bore, however, no proportion to his ample poſſeſſions: on the contrary, though profuſe in the gratification of his appetites, he was accuſed by the popular voice of an attention to the arts of œconomy, unworthy of his high birth and ſplendid fortune. Emulous of being thought to reſemble Henry the Fourth, and the Regent Duke of Orleans, from both of which Princes he derived his deſcent, he had no ſimilarity to either, except in the foibles which ſhaded the character of the former, and in the vices which diſgraced the conduct of the latter. The beneficence, the heroic valour, and clemency of mind, which characteriſed the King of Navarre, were not to be traced

in

in his degenerate grandson. The sublime talents, the military genius, and the various endowments of a statesman and a general, which combined in the Regent, were as vainly sought in the Duke of Orleans.

Abandoned to pleasures of every description, he yet had no elevation nor refinement in his amusements. His personal courage, which had sustained some injury, and excited some sarcastic comments, from his behaviour under d'Orvilliers in 1778, had not been retrieved by his unpropitious attempt to signalize himself, by accompanying Charles and Robert into the air. The malignant reflexions formerly thrown out upon his intrepidity as a naval officer, were followed by pasquinades upon his supposed apprehensions in the balloon; and he was said to have been as unfortunate in the park of Meudon, where he alighted from his aerial excursion, as he had been at an earlier period of his life, in the vicinity of the islands of Ushant. Notwithstanding

ing thefe afperfions and defects, he yet poffeffed qualities, which if conducted by judgment, might have redeemed him from the load of obloquy under which he was oppreffed. His talents were certainly above mediocrity; his mind enlarged, his manners condefcending and popular, and his underftanding cultivated by letters; and an extenfive acquaintance with mankind.

He was the only Prince of the Houfe of Bourbon who had ever vifited England in perfon; the Duke d'Alençon, brother to Henry the Third of France, having been the laft, who in the profecution of his defign to marry Elizabeth, had paffed over into thefe kingdoms. The diforders in the finances, and the defperate, or arbitrary meafures to which the Court was neceffitated perpetually to have recourfe, in order to raife new loans and obtain fupplies, had given the Duke of Orleans an occafion, of which he gladly availed himfelf, to regain his long loft popularity. To this public and oftenfible caufe of his alienation from the Court, were added

L   fome

some private misunderstandings, which had their origin in the interference of the Queen to prevent an alliance, which was projected between the eldest son of the Count d'Artois, and the daughter of the Duke of Orleans: a marriage which it was more than possible might eventually elevate the young Princess to the Throne of France. Animated and stimulated by these motives, he seemed to awake from the dissolute pleasures in which he had been plunged, and to assume the more dignified and ingratiating character of an opposer of despotism, and a protector of the people. This change of conduct soon produced its full effect; and he passed with the most rapid transition, from the contempt and reprobation of the inhabitants of Paris, to the heighth of favour and general attachment.

Such was the aspect which the Court of Versailles presented at the commencement of the year 1787, and such were the principal characters and personages of which it was composed. The sources of discontent,
and

and even of revolt and infurrection, were numerous and augmenting. The ordinary channels of revenue were either dried up, or had become inadequate to the exigencies of the Government. Recourfe was therefore reluctantly had to other modes of obtaining fupplies; and the convocation of the "Notables" was propofed by Calonne to the King, and adopted immediately, as the only remaining expedient.

In thefe critical circumftances of perplexity and diftrefs, Vergennes, whofe high reputation and fuperior talents had hitherto diffufed a luftre over the councils of France, and alone fuftained the tottering load of public credit and national grandeur: this celebrated Minifter, the fucceffor of Maurepas, and who, fince his death, had during eight years held the firft place in the Adminiftration, was removed by death from a fcene, to which all his abilities would probably have been found unequal. Fortunate in his alliances, in his wars, in his negociations, in his acquifition of fame, in the enjoyment of the royal favour and the popular opinion, he was yet more happy in not furviving thefe frail and uncertain poffeffions. Unlike to Louvois and to Fleury, he neither forfeited the affection of his Sovereign, nor outlived his own talents and capacity. Admired, regretted, and lamented, his death feemed to be the fignal which unloofed the jarring elements of civil commotion, and which marked the æra of the extinction of tranquillity and obedience.

The difmiffion of Calonne followed in a few weeks; and the elevation of an ecclefiaftic, the Archbifhop of Touloufe, to the fupreme controul of the finances, whatever expectations it might at firft awaken of alleviation and redrefs, only tended in the event to aggravate the national calamities, and to encreafe the popular difcontent. New fyftems, equally unproductive as the preceding, and only calculated for temporary relief, afforded neither a remedy to the preffing neceffities of the court, nor to the clamorous griev-

ances

ances of the people. The "Notables" were found to be equally incompetent and averſe, to adduce any cure for theſe multiplied diſtempers of the ſtate. They were therefore diſſolved; and the nation already began to demand an aſſembly of the " States General," as the laſt and only meaſure competent to extricate and retrieve them from the danger of impending bankruptcy and ruin.

But the troubles and internal feuds of the Dutch commonwealth, which had been long nouriſhed and fed by the political liberality of the cabinet of Verſailles; which had grown up under the foſtering hand of Vergennes, and which a ſeries of deep and artful negociations had inflamed and augmented, now approached rapidly to their criſis. Never could they have attained to their maturity at a more inauſpicious moment for France; and never was the triumph of fortune over the machinations of policy more conſpicuouſly exemplified.

William

William the Fifth, Prince of Orange, poſſeſſed the Stadtholderate of the United Provinces. Allied by name rather than by blood, to the great Houſe of Naſſau, ſo fertile in heroes and in legiſlators, few traces of the ſublime qualities which have rendered that family immortal, were to be diſcovered in their ſucceſſor. But, in the Princeſs his wife, ſprung from the union of the houſes of Brandenburgh and Naſſau, the characteriſtic energy of both was viſible. Driven out of the Province of Holland by the indignities and inſults with which the republican faction had treated the Prince, whom they had compelled to retire to Nimeguen, ſhe had the courage to ſet out for the Hague, and, unattended by any guards, to traverſe a hoſtile country, in the hope of adjuſting by her preſence, addreſs, and flexibility, the points in diſpute between her huſband and the States. In this arduous and delicate attempt ſhe was fruſtrated, and even her perſon laid under an arreſt, by the brutality of one of the military officers

in

in the service of the Republic. Obliged to abandon her project, and to return to Nimeguen, she invoked the protection and assistance of the King of Prussia, to re-instate the exiled Stadtholder in the hereditary dignities and offices, of which he had been so unjustly and unconstitutionally deprived. It was not to her uncle that she addressed these entreaties. The great Frederick was no more: he had paid the common tribute to mortality, and had expired at Potzdam under the accumulating weight of age and diseases. But, though he no longer animated in person the councils of Berlin, the vigour of his genius survived: it seemed even to have attained new force in the hands of a Sovereign, whose more active period of life led him to adopt measures of decision, and whose near relationship to the Princess of Orange stimulated him to warmer exertions in her behalf.

The juncture was favourable to the Prussian interposition; and England, under the auspices of a Minister prompt to seize

seize the occasion of again re-appearing with dignity and effect on the Continent, avowedly joined and aided the attack upon the enemies of the house of Orange. An army of about fifteen thousand men, commanded by the first military genius in Europe, the Duke of Brunswick, entered the territories of the States General, in September, 1787, and over-ran with the same rapidity that Louis the Fourteenth had done in last century, the province of Holland. Amsterdam itself, the centre of disaffection, and the last asylum of the French and republican factions, after a short and ineffectual struggle, capitulated, and received the conqueror. A complete, but almost bloodless revolution was effected; and the Hague, so long a prey to discord and to animosity, saw the Stadtholder return, and occupy his high station, with every expression of loyalty and attachment.

France, embarrassed, and incapable from her domestic misfortunes, of interfering either with honour to herself, or efficacy to her

her friends, though she appeared to make a feeble effort in their favour, yet ultimately gave way to the storm, and consented to disarm; nay more, publicly to deny her having ever intended to sustain that party, in whose support she had expended her treasures, and for whom, in more auspicious æras, she would have involved Europe in blood and hostility. The high reputation which so signal a success reflected on the councils of Great Britain, was contrasted and rendered more splendid, by a comparison with the fallen state of her ancient rival, who, only a few years preceding these events, in conjunction with America, had seemed to give laws in every quarter of the globe. The energy and wise precaution of the Minister did not, however, remit its vigilance, or content itself with having liberated the Dutch Republic, and reinstated the Stadtholder. Attentive to profit of this fortunate and propitious moment, and to avail himself of the gratitude with which the assistance extended to Holland had equally impressed

impressed the Government and the people, he cemented those sentiments by immediately framing, and eventually concluding a defensive treaty with the United Provinces. It was signed in April, 1788, and was evidently built on the model of that, which had been terminated under the auspices of Vergennes, between France and Holland, towards the close of the year 1785. Reciprocal succours, naval and military, were stipulated; and the bands of political union were drawn as close, as human wisdom and mutual interest could devise.

This alliance, so much approved, and so highly beneficial to England, was succeeded by a second, similar in its tenor, nature, and tendency, between the Courts of St. James's and Berlin, which was ratified in the month of August of the same year. They had been preceded by a subsidiary treaty between England and the Landgrave of Hesse, which enabled the former power, on the payment of a certain annual sum, to demand from the latter,

latter, at a very fhort notice, a body of twelve thoufand troops.

Thus, in the fpace of only four years which might be faid to have elapfed fince the complete triumph of the Sovereign and the nation over the " Coalition," had Great Britain, under the conduct of a Minifter who had not yet attained his thirtieth year, rifen from a ftate of unexampled depreffion, to her antient fuperiority among the European kingdoms. The finances had been re-eftablifhed by a fyftem of unremitting and fevere œconomy. Commerce, aided and emancipated by the wife regulations of an enlarged policy, opened new fources, and navigated feas hitherto unknown or unexplored, in the profecution of its objects. Public credit attained a point of elevation and permanence, unparelleled fince the commencement of the unfortunate war with America. The councils of England, conducted on principles, not of a crooked duplicity, but of rectitude and magnanimity, excited refpect and approbation in the furrounding states,

states, while they diffused prosperity and felicity over every part of the island.

Political alliances and connections on the Continent, added the prospect of stability to every measure which was calculated for internal security or commercial advantage. The calamities of Lord North's Administration, and the anarchy which succeeded that unfortunate period: the defalcation of thirteen provinces, and of both the Floridas from the empire: the disgraces of Saratoga, and of the Chesapeake: the tumults, and conflagration of London: in a word, the varied and accumulated misfortunes, which for a long series of years oppressed, and had almost overwhelmed the commonwealth, were already erased from the recollection. A mild and happy calm had smoothed these troubled waves. The Sovereign was deservedly dear to every rank and order of his subjects, who united in regarding him as their father and benefactor. The Government, beloved at home, was respected abroad; and the people, happy beyond the example of former

former times, looked up with equal affection and veneration towards the fource of thefe multiplied benefits.

But in the midſt of this flattering aſpect of affairs, an unexpected and difaſtrous change was preparing to manifeſt itſelf, which no human prudence could have forefeen, or precautions delayed. We were deſtined to experience in its fulleſt extent, the mutability of fortune, and the fragility of greatneſs; to hold out a memorable leſſon to our own, and to future times, that the fplendor and felicity of man, however folid the foundations on which they may feem to repoſe, are in the hands of a fuperior Being, who confers, or withdraws them in an inſtant. I am arrived at that awful and affecting period, when the feelings of all thofe who ſhall peruſe theſe ſheets, will anticipate my own; and which, from a variety of motives, I ſhould wiſh to cover under a veil of oblivion, if the publicity of the great leading facts, and ſtill more, if the inſtruction conveyed by the narration itſelf,

as

as one of the most interesting portions of modern annals, did not supercede my personal inclinations. It is not, however, either in my plan or my intention, to relate the *private* history of that extraordinary period; or to drag into daylight facts and anecdotes, which, curious and entertaining as they must appear to posterity, are, in every sense, unfit for the perusal of the present age. Sentiments of duty, delicacy, and respect towards a Prince inexpressibly dear to his people; towards a Queen, who during near thirty years, and in every relation of domestic life, has been blameless and exemplary: towards those illustrious persons, on whom the sceptre of George the Third must, in the ordinary progress of events, at some future, and as we trust, far distant period, devolve: even motives of prudence, decorum, and propriety, arrest my pen; and prevent me from shading a picture, the outline only of which it is either wise or necessary to hold up to the public eye, placed as we are so near the object.

 The very nature of the subject is, indeed, such

such as to add peculiar embarrassments to those general ones, which present themselves in the way of every man who shall venture to relate the transactions of the time in which he lives, and of which he forms himself, though an imperceptible, yet a real and efficient part. Nor is it even a sufficient justification or inducement to undertake such a task, that the mild genius of the century in which we write, or the freedom which enables us to dictate without apprehension, appear to liberate us from every restraint. There are feelings in a generous mind, anterior to all written law, and far superior in their operation to those regulations which are imposed by Courts of Judicature, or legislative bodies. It is to these restrictions that I shall subject my pen, while the great chain of events may yet be presented to the English people, and the fidelity of historical truth be preserved inviolate. "Ut, non modo casus, eventusque rerum, qui plerumque fortuiti sunt, sed ratio etiam, causæque noscantur." Like the sublime writer whom I have just cited, and who flourished under the golden reign

reign of Trajan, we too, "rara temporum felicitate, ubi fentire quæ velis, et quæ fentias dicere licet," may, unawed by power, affix the fentiment of approbation and of cenfure, in conformity to our own conviction. Such is equally my defign and my determination. But it is only for thofe who can elevate their minds above the little partialities and prejudices of the day, that it belongs to appreciate the performance of this promife; and to decide how far the prefent work may venture to lay claim to any portion of Roman energy and freedom, or how far the immortal writings of antiquity would be fullied and degraded by a comparifon with this production.

It is not eafy to imagine or to parallel in the hiftory of the prefent century, a period of more perfect ferenity than that which England prefented in the autumn of 1788. The King, accompanied by the Queen, and furrounded by his family, after having tried the effects of a relaxation from public bufinefs, and of the medi-

cinal

cinal waters of Cheltenham, had returned to Windsor; not, indeed, in a state of vigorous health, but by no means in any such declining state of indisposition, as to excite alarm among his subjects. The Prince of Wales, as usual, passed the summer at his Marine Pavillion at Brighthelmstone. Mr. Pitt, occupied in the functions of his station, was detained in the vicinity of the capital; while Mr. Fox, whose faculties of body and mind had been not a little exercised and exhausted, by a toilsome attendance in Covent Garden during the extreme heats of August, which was thought requisite to secure the election of Lord John Townsend as member for Westminster; indulged a degree of necessary repose, and withdrew for a short time from the hurry of political life. He quitted England, and repaired to Switzerland and Italy, as a scene calculated to amuse and entertain, while it restored and invigorated a constitution, impaired by constant exertion. The great leaders of Ministry and Opposition, having laid aside their political animosities, were dispersed in peaceful inactivity over every part of the kingdom. From this state of public recreation and felicity, the nation was rudely and suddenly awoke, by the reports of his Majesty being attacked with an unexpected and dangerous illness. The precise nature of it was for several days unascertained and unexplained, even to those whose residence near the court should have enabled them to obtain early and authentic information. Meanwhile, fame augmented the evil, and the death of the Sovereign was believed to have either already taken place, or to be imminent and inevitable.

The grief and distraction which were manifested in every part of the island, on the publication of this calamitous event, can be only compared with that of the Roman people, on the news of Germanicus being seized with mortal symptoms at Antioch; as the distressful situation of the Queen bore some resemblance to that of Agrippina.

"Passim

"Paſſim ſilentia et gemitus, nihil compoſitum in oſtentationem; et quanquam neque inſignibus lugentium abſtinerent, altius animis mœrebant." Time, however, gradually divulged the truth, and changed the apprehenſions of the nation for the ſituation of the King. His diſorder was underſtood to have fallen upon the brain, and to have produced, as might be expected, a temporary privation of reaſon. As the cauſe of this alienation of mind was extraneous and violent, it might be hoped that it could only be of ſhort duration: but the iſſue was uncertain, while the ſuſpenſion of all government, and of every function attached to the kingly dignity, was immediate and indiſputable. A ſpecies of interregnum in fact took place; though unaccompanied by any of thoſe circumſtances, which uſually characterize and accompany that unfortunate ſtate. The kingdom, anxious, and with eyes directed towards their Sovereign, betrayed no ſymptoms of confuſion, anarchy, or civil commotion. The Firſt Miniſter continued to exercife,

cife, by a general submission and consent, the powers delegated to him before the King's indisposition; and the political machine, well constructed, and properly organized, sustained no derangement or injury whatsoever from this shock, except those inseparably connected with delay in the transactions or negociations pending with foreign courts.

Meanwhile, the Heir to the monarchy had quitted Brighthelmstone on the first information of his father's malady, and repaired to Windsor, whither he was followed by the Duke of York. Physicians were called in, though ineffectually; and as the nature of the distemper and of its final termination opened a wide field to conjecture, change and alteration, an express was sent to overtake Mr. Fox in whatever part of the Continent he might be found; and to intreat that he would return without delay to England.

The two Houses of Parliament, in consequence of the preceding prorogation, met in a few days subsequent to these extraordinary

traordinary events. The general agitation and curiosity, even if they had not been aided by other emotions of hope and fear, of ambition, and of public duty, would alone have produced a numerous attendance. Mr. Pitt opened the subject of their meeting in a very concise and pathetic manner; lamented the occasion, expressed his hope that the cause would speedily be removed, and in pursuance of that idea, advised an immediate adjournment of a fortnight. The proposition was received in deep silence by the opposite side of the House, and assented to in mute acquiescence. Their leader was not yet arrived; and consequently time was wanted to adjust and determine on their plan of action, under circumstances so delicate and unprecedented. In the interval which took place, his Majesty was removed to the palace of Kew. The Prince of Wales returned to Carlton House; and Mr. Fox, impatiently expected, after a journey which he performed with incredible expedition from Bologna, in a very infirm

and

and difordered ftate of health, arrived in London, and affumed his juft pre-eminence in the counfels of his party.

Thofe counfels evinced their nature and object, as foon as the late adjournment was at an end; and Mr. Fox, generoufly, though perhaps injudicioufly ftepping forward in the fenate, rather laid claim to the vacant fceptre in the name and on the behalf of the Heir Apparent, as belonging and devolving to him of right; than preferred his pretenfions with modefty and fubmiffion, at the bar of the affembled nation. Perhaps a ftep more injurious to the great perfonage whom it was intended to ferve, or more pregnant with confequences to be deprecated, of every kind, could not have been devifed or executed. Perhaps, too, when time fhall have withdrawn that curtain which is ftill ftretched acrofs thefe recent and interefting events, we may difcover, that in advancing fo unqualified a demand of the regency, he did not precifely follow the dictates of his own elevated mind, and illuminated judgment.

It

It wakened a jealous spirit of enquiry into the supposed origin and foundation of that asserted right, in the breasts even of the most liberal and unprejudiced. It compelled Administration to probe that problematical and obscure part of the British Constitution. It reminded those, to whom the writings of Shakespear were familiar, of that affecting and pathetic scene, where Henry the Fourth, under a temporary privation of his faculties, finds on his recovery, that his eldest son has carried away the insignia of his royal dignity, which, had he only waited a few hours, would have been his by devolution.

The discernment of Mr. Pitt saw, and instantly enabled him to profit of this error in his antagonist. He demanded the discussion and decision of so great and leading a principle, which led to conclusions unlimited and undefined, as well as subversive of the tenure on which a King of England had originally received his crown; previous to any ulterior disposition and distribution of offices. He was joined by by the majority of the House in this requisition, and thus commenced his resistance under auspices and circumstances peculiarly fortunate. It was in vain that the Prince of Wales, already rendered sensible of the injury which his cause had sustained, equally in Parliament and among the people, by Mr. Fox's unqualified claim of right, endeavoured to wave and prevent all further discussion of so invidious a subject. It was in vain that the Duke of York, in his brother's name, and by his authority, renounced any such assumption of power, and made this public declaration in the House of Lords. Nor was Mr. Fox's attempt to qualify his first assertion, and to give it a more mitigated sense, received with better success in the other House. Parliament, roused to a sense of the necessity of declaring itself solely competent to fill the vacant throne, proceeded to that great act without circumlocution or delay; and having pronounced upon this important preliminary, then decided that the Prince of Wales should

should be invited and requested to accept the Regency, under certain limitations. The month of December elapsed in these contests, and the year 1789 commenced under the most gloomy presages. Mutual asperity and reproach embittered every debate. No appearances of convalescence or recovery, so ardently anticipated by the nation, had yet manifested themselves in the malady of the King. In addition to the keenest sensations of private distress as a mother and a wife, the Queen saw herself on the point of being placed in the most painful, though indispensably necessary situation; that of being entrusted with the care of the Royal Person, and of standing in a sort of rivality and competition to her eldest son. The Prince, who aspired to a Regency, unfettered by any restrictions, betrayed in his reply to a letter which the First Minister addressed to him, and in which the great features of that intended delegation of the Royal power were delineated, his warm resentment and dissatisfaction at many of those defalcations.

He concluded, however, by reluctantly and coldly confenting to receive it, curtailed and degraded as it might be by Minifterial or Parliamentary diftruft.

A fecond examination of the phyficians who had attended his Majefty during the courfe of his diforder, which took place before a Committee of the Houfe of Commons, and which was certainly not conducted on the part of Oppofition with either delicacy or judgment, tended to throw very little light on the great object of public enquiry; the probable duration and period of this afflicting malady. Mr. Pitt conftantly and warmly maintained the probability of its happy termination; and regarding it as neither diftant nor hopelefs, made the refumption of the Royal power by the Sovereign with facility and celerity, as foon as he fhould be enabled to wield the fceptre, the firft and leading principle of all his meafures and propofitions. The adherents of the Prince of Wales faw the profpect of his father's recovery through a very different medium, and conceived of it not only as improbable,

ble, but as hourly augmenting in that improbability. They were sustained in this opinion by Warren, as the Minister was confirmed in his opposite sentiment by Willis; two physicians, on whose contradictory prognostics and apprehensions each party implicitly relied. The former, at the summit of his profession, and unquestionably possessed of great medical skill, was yet accused by the public voice of leaning in his inclination towards the party of the Prince. The latter, brought from a distant province to attend the Sovereign under his severe disorder, and having been peculiarly conversant in that species of disease, boldly and early asserted that he entertained scarcely any doubts of the King's perfect re-establishment at no remote period. The event fully justified his prediction.

Meanwhile the introduction of the propositions upon which the Regency Bill was meant to be founded, and the restrictions intended to be imposed upon the power of the future Regent, which were brought forward by the First Minister in the House of Commons, carried the rage and virulence of party to its utmost height. The negation of the power of creating Peers: the nomination of a council to assist the Queen: and the complete reservation of the Royal household, were all arraigned and condemned in the warmest terms by Mr. Fox, as dictated only by ambition, and not originating in state necessity, or even in regard to the situation of the Monarch. The history of France under the unhappy reign of Charles the Sixth, was cited, as bearing a manifest resemblance to the present disastrous period; and a Queen, equally venerated and beloved by the nation, was compared to the unnatural Isabella of Bavaria; as her son the Dauphin's abandoned and persecuted state was asserted to be similar to that of the Prince of Wales. Unmoved by these invectives, and sustained by conscious rectitude of intention, the Minister steadily pursued his way: nor was he, in this critical and distressing moment,

deserted

deserted by either House of Parliament. The Chancellor, who, at the commencement of the King's illness, had been supposed to have listened to proposals for forming a part of a new Administration; anxious to evince the falsehood of so unjust an aspersion, and to give the most unequivocal proofs of loyalty and of adherence to his Sovereign under the present circumstances, collected all the energy of his mind in the various appeals, which he successfully made to the honour and patriotism of the House of Lords.

In this stage of the public business, at a moment when the King's situation appeared most to exclude hope, and while the House of Commons were fully occupied in framing the principal component parts of the act which was to establish the Regency, Mr. Fox withdrew from the scene, and quitting London, retired to Bath. His disordered state of health was assigned as a pretext for this secession at so extraordinary and critical a juncture; but the public conceived the motives of it to originate in very different

different causes. Dissention and jealousy had already pervaded the counsels of Carlton House. The distribution of offices under the approaching Regency had produced alienation among the chiefs. An interior Cabinet, different in its views, and opposite in its objects to the great ostensible leaders of the party attached to the Prince of Wales, had set up a separate standard, and formed a distinct interest. Difference of opinion had manifested itself upon some very delicate, and personal points. Cabal and intrigue had penetrated into the closet. His Royal Highness was generally supposed to have experienced difficulties, if not peremptory refusals of gratifying his wishes, on the part of the Duke of Portland; and that, in relation to persons and things peculiarly near his heart. These numerous sources of disunion were still however, in some measure concealed from view, by their very nature, and the mutual interest or honour of the parties themselves. The great acts of parliamentary legislation proceeded,
and

and were nearly approaching to their termination. A very short period, probably not exceeding three days, must have completed the bill, which was to declare the incapacity of the Sovereign to conduct the national affairs, and to transfer the sceptre, though with diminished influence, to his son. The members of Administration were on the point of resigning their charges, and the new Ministry, already settled, prepared to enter on office; while the English people, fondly attached by every sense of loyalty and affection to their Monarch, as well as from gratitude and esteem to the First Minister, in dejection and silence looked on, and saw the Government transferred to others, who, whatever abilities they might collectively possess, certainly neither merited nor enjoyed the general approbation and confidence.

But the term of interregnum and misfortune was now arrived; and the impending calamity which had menaced England with all the evils of a Regency,

far

far more to be deprecated and dreaded than those from which the country had escaped in 1784, was suddenly and unexpectedly dissipated. The disorder, under which the King had suffered during three months, and whose violence had hitherto appeared to baffle all medical skill and exertion, gradually, but rapidly subsided. Sanity of mind and reason resumed their seat, and left no trace of their temporary subversion. Time confirmed the cure, and restored to his subjects a Prince, rendered supremely and peculiarly dear to them by the recent prospect and apprehension of his loss. The vision of a Regency faded and disappeared, as the Sovereign came forward to public view, and was totally extinguished by his resumption of all the regal functions. The demonstrations of national joy far exceeded any recorded in the English annals, and were probably more real and unfeigned than ever were offered on similar occasions. It was not only that a King, beloved and respected, was recovered from the most afflicting of

all

all situations incident to humanity, and enabled to re-ascend the throne. Sentiments of disapprobation and of general condemnation, affixed to the measures and conduct of the opposite party, heightened the emotions of pleasure, by a comparison with that state from which the kingdom had been so fortunately delivered. No efforts of despotism, or mandates of absolute power could have produced the illuminations, which the capital exhibited in testimony of its loyalty; and these proofs of attachment were renewed, and even augmented, on the occasion of his Majesty's first appearance in public, and his solemn procession to St. Paul's, to return thanks to Heaven for his recovery. Serenity and tranquillity, so long banished, resumed their place, and soon effaced the recollection of a calamity, not more awful and alarming in its appearance and progress, than speedily and happily extinguished.

The attention of Europe, which had been so powerfully attracted towards England during the continuance of the severe indisposition

sition of George the Third, was now to be directed to another object scarcely less productive of change, and big with the most important consequences. France, so long inured to servitude, and only tracing the existence of her liberties in the page of forgotten historians, or antiquaries: whose fetters, originally imposed by Richlieu, and strengthened by Mazarin, had been rivetted by the lapse of near two centuries; by the proud tyranny of Louis the Fourteenth, and by the profligate despotism of his successor: France, stimulated by the writings of genius and philosophy, which in defiance of arbitrary power, have illuminated and dignified the present age, aspired to freedom. The weakness of the Sovereign; the incapacity or timidity of his Ministers; the exhausted state of the treasury and finances; the unexampled and pertinacious opposition of the Parliament of Paris to register, or sanction the Royal edicts for the imposition of new taxes; the failure of the harvests, and consequent augmentation in the price of bread; all

these

these concurring circumstances contributed to produce and accelerate a revolution.

The various Parliaments of the kingdom, in terms of energy and firmness to which they had been long disused, clamorously demanded the immediate convocation of the "States General," as the only constitutional, or adequate remedy to the distempers of the state. They adhered to this requisition, not only in defiance of the displeasure of the Crown, which was manifested by the banishment of the Parliament of Paris to Troyes in Champagne; but in opposition to their own essential interests, and even eventual existence. The nobility, attached by so many ties to the Sovereign, and the natural supporters of his prerogative; irritated at the attempt made by Calonne, and persisted in by the Archbishop of Toulouse, to deprive them of their exemption from the projected land tax, or "impot territorial," joined the courts of judicature in their refusal to register the measures proposed, and forsook their hereditary maxims of policy, to adopt the popular party. The irrefolute conduct of the Firft Minifter under thefe delicate and trying circumftances, invigorated and emboldened the enemies of Government; and the fpirit of remonftrance, complaint, and menace, defseminated with induftry, became daily more general and alarming.

The Archbifhop, after many inefficient or unfuccefsful plans for the re-eftablifhment of the finances, and fome ill-conceived exertions of feverity and power againft his opponents, felt himfelf unequal to combat the gathering ftorm of national indignation; and retiring from a fituation of danger and eminence, abandoned his mafter to the mercy of events. He even quitted France, and pafsed the Alps into Italy; as Calonne, under fimilar expreffions of general refentment, had done in the preceding year; when finding the Royal protection withdrawn, and already impeached by the Parliament of Paris, he retreated firft into Holland, and from thence crofsed the fea to England. In this perplexed fituation, Louis the Sixteenth

teenth, compelled to difmifs one Minifter, and forfaken by another; furrounded with embarraffments, and having only a choice of evils; confcious that the very foundations of the throne and monarchy were crumbling under his feet; endowed with no talents or great qualities which might enable him to fuftain his own dignity, coerce his fubjects, or reftore order and energy in the public affairs: alarmed and terrified at the demonftrations of difcontent which appeared in the capital, and the provinces: under the preffure of thefe various confiderations and apprehenfions, he embraced the refolution of meeting the wifhes of the nation; and if driven to the laft neceffity, of laying the diftreffes of the Crown before the reprefentatives of the people.

Neckar, who had conducted the finances during the profecution of the late war with England, and who had attained a very unmerited degree of popularity fince his difmiffion from office, was reinftated in his employment of Comptroller General. The avowed enemy of Calonne, whom

he

he accufed of peculation and malverfation, he had appealed to the public by various controverfial writings, defamatory of that Minifter, and tending to criminate him as a defaulter in the eyes of France and of all Europe. The famous "Compte rendu au Roi" in 1781, in which he laid open to his own Sovereign, and to all mankind, the expenditure, revenue, and refources of his country, may be regarded not only as an unprecedented difclofure of the hitherto facred and unrevealed arcana of the French monarchy; but as having operated much beyond the immediate and oftenfible pretext of his own juftification; by awakening, and directing the reflexions of every clafs of men towards the profufe diftribution of the public treafure. Simple in his exterior, and decent in his manners, Neckar attained the fame of difintereftednefs and probity. Equally republican in birth and in principles, he flattered by thefe circumftances, the prevailing fpirit and genius of the times. Avowedly odious to the party of the Queen, and

of

of the Count d'Artois, he could hardly be supposed to possess the real confidence or attachment of the King, who had only been driven by his own distress, and the current of popular favor, to have recourse to his assistance and services. Deficient in all the essential qualities of a great Minister, and ignorant of those enlarged principles of taxation and revenue, which were alone competent to the extrication of so vast a monarchy as France, he supplied these defects by little arts and narrow projects, adapted to the exigencies of the day. In the Canton of Bern his talents might have entitled him to respect, and they would have been in their proper sphere. An able arithmetician, but a feeble statesman, he only appeared in the first station of finance, to evince how inadequate were his abilities to that dangerous elevation; and after vainly attempting to sustain an ill-founded reputation, he has now retired to oblivion, unlamented, and almost unnoticed by that nation, among whom he was so lately idolized.

Although

Although the recall and nomination of Neckar appeared to give general satisfaction, and awakened the hopes of his numerous and sanguine admirers, yet these symptoms of approbation gradually subsided. The temporary effect of his name in raising the public credit, produced no permanent or beneficial consequence. Languor and debility characterized every operation of finance; and Government became less competent to resist the encroachments of the people, in proportion as its embarrassment multiplied. Paris, rendered clamorous by the high price of grain, and attributing this scarcity more to the arts of monopoly, and even to the indirect interference of the Court in permitting the exportation of corn, than to any deficiency in the productions of the earth, proceeded to acts of violence, bordering on insurrection. The introduction of a body of military forces into the capital, quelled, not without a considerable effusion of blood, these first symptoms of revolt, and restored a degree of tranquillity and submission. Notwithstanding this apparent check to the spirit of popular innovation, every circumstance tended to evince, that the numerous subjects of complaint on the side of the People could not be extinguished, by any expedient short of unconditional submission on the part of the Crown; or of an appeal to the sword, if the former measure should be thought too degrading for a Prince born in the purple, and accustomed to regard his power as unlimited and irresistible. The naked and unprotected Majesty of the throne, no longer environed, as under Louis the Fourteenth, by a splendid household and the pomp of royalty, formed a very inefficient barrier against a nation, enthusiastic in their demands of a constitution; and who seemed to be determined to seize the favourable moment, for curtailing the odious prerogative of issuing " Lettres de Cachet," and raising supplies by arbitrary mandate. The levities and profusion of the Queen; the haughty tone which was assumed by the Count d'Artois on several occasions; and the supposed subservience of the King to his wife and brother, encreased the frenzy for reformation, and added to the general effervescence. Yielding with ungracious reluctance to these manifestations of the approaching storm, the King consented to adopt the humiliating and unwelcome advice offered by his Minister, of convoking the States General at Versailles: but, at the same time, stimulated to resistance by his own feelings, as well as by the exhortations of those who were continually near his person, he began to prepare for extremities, and to assemble forces.

The Duke of Orleans, who, at an early period of the present troubles, had been ordered to retire to his seat at Reinsy, on account of the active part which he had taken in opposition to the Government, had obtained, from the lenity or indulgence of the Court, permission to revisit Paris. Less sensible to this mark of favour, than irritated by the act of severity which preceded it, he determined on revenge, and embraced with ardor the popular cause. His high quality and near alliance to the

the Sovereign; his immense revenues; his central situation at the "Palais Royal," in the heart of the metropolis; his numerous connexions, and extensive influence: this combination of circumstances enabled him to become a very dangerous and formidable opponent to the Crown, in its present fallen and debilitated state. He probably did not apprehend the extremities to which his own intrigues might conduct a tumultuous assembly; or he might conceive that he should always be able to direct its operations, and to superintend its movements. It is even possible, as his enemies assert, that the flattering prospect of the Regency, which already opened itself to his ambition as neither a remote nor improbable event, conduced to determine his line of action, and to prevent him from seeing the precipices with which such a pursuit was surrounded. He was elected a member of the States General for Crepy in Valois, and took his seat in the Assembly.

This extraordinary convocation of all the orders of the kingdom, which had not been summoned since the Regency of Mary of Medicis, and whose very existence seemed to have been annihilated by three long reigns of arbitrary power, was opened with the utmost solemnity by Louis the Sixteenth, assisted by the Princes of the Blood, and accompanied with all the external splendor becoming so august a ceremony. Many sources of internal discord and confusion, almost inevitable from the competition and opposite pretensions or interest of the Nobility, Clergy, and Third Estate; the facility of introducing corruption among so vast and mixed a body of men; above all, the loyalty and adherence naturally to be expected from the two first classes of the states: these inherent vices in their formation inspired the Court with a confidence, that no unanimity or exertion of vigour would ever characterize so heterogeneous a mass. The first proceedings of the Assembly justified these expectations. Much time elapsed in disputes arising from the incompatibility of the respective demands of the different orders; and though

these

these were at last happily terminated by the Nobility and Clergy renouncing, or acquiescing in the claims of the delegates of the people; yet the Sovereign still possessed great resources, and various means of protracting or averting any act militating vitally against his prerogatives.

Had Louis the Sixteenth been left to the impulse and direction of his own character, it is probable that he would have continued to yield to the encroachments of the democratical spirit, which had already produced so many involuntary concessions on the part of the Crown; and which, encreasing in vigour as it proceeded, avowedly aimed at giving birth to a free constitution, and a limited monarchy. He wanted all that energy, elevation, and courage requisite to sustain him in a struggle against his people, and to enable him to repress their attempts at emancipation. But in the Queen and the Count d'Artois, resentment at the inroads of a nation whom they had long regarded only as formed for servitude; and the habitual exercise of arbitrary power,

warmly

warmly impelled to every exertion for its preservation; while it dictated the most decided measures for repressing and chastizing a mutinous and discontented capital.

They united their efforts to sustain the irresolution of the King, and succeeded. It was determined in the cabinet of Versailles, to adopt the most vigorous principles; to dissolve the National Assembly; to dismiss the Comptroller-General; and to punish the insolence of the metropolis. Prudence and address were, however, requisite to mature these counsels, and to facilitate their execution. A great body of forces, principally consisting of the Swiss and German regiments in the service of France, was gradually collected from different provinces. The Marechal de Broglio, an officer of high military reputation, and of known attachment to the Crown, was named to the supreme command. Every necessary preparation for maintaining the Royal authority, if necessary, by the most spirited and severe acts of punishment, was made, without even

the

affectation of disguise or concealment. The capital, incapable of resistance, and unconscious even of its own capacities of defence; destitute of leaders, of arms, and of troops, waited patiently the chastizement which impended.

Paris, involved in circumstances more distressful even than those in which it stood, when invested by Henry the Third in 1589, and under an equal necessity of submitting to the conditions which an incensed monarch might have dictated, was snatched from pillage by a revolution not less sudden and unexpected, than that which, two centuries preceding, had deprived Henry the Third of his life. The frantic and sanguinary zeal of a Monk affected this deliverance in one instance: in the other, the Parisians were indebted to the timidity, delays, and want of decision in the Court. During the first days of July, the metropolis, though turbulent and riotous, made no exertions to oppose the army by which it was encircled and surrounded. The partizans and supporters of the Royal power were numerous, and

ready

ready to evince their zeal and loyalty. The "Prevot des Marchands," who is the first municipal magistrate, was in the interests of the Crown. The Bastile awed one part of the capital, as the "Hotel des Invalides" did the other. Paris, taken in the toils of arbitrary power, might have been disarmed, and deprived of the means to excite future commotion. The imprudence, pusillanimity, and impatience of the Court rendered these advantages of no avail, and precipitated the unfortunate Prince upon measures which terminated in irremediable disgrace and ruin.

Mistaking, or neglecting the most obvious principles of policy and wise precaution, which dictated to commence the plan of operations by subjecting Paris, from whence alone any danger was to be apprehended; the King was induced to dismiss Neckar with expressions of indignation, which were accompanied by menaces and insult on the part of his brother, the Count d'Artois. This step, which evinced a total change of resolutions, and which,

from

from the popularity of the Minister, was likely to produce a violent fermentation in every order of men, was followed by others equally injudicious. The States General were driven into the "Salle des Etats" where they held their meetings, by detachments of the Guards; who surrounded them, and who waited only the orders of the Court, to proceed to greater extremities against the obnoxious representatives of the nation.

Had these manifestations of vigour been only sustained by instantly attacking and entering Paris, it is not to be doubted that, unprepared as it still was, and unwilling to expose to the licence of an incensed soldiery the lives and properties of its citizens, the capital would have been without difficulty reduced to obedience. But, an ill-timed and fatal delay, equally injurious with the preceding precipitation, gave the inhabitants time to recover from their first emotions of surprize and apprehension. They saw the timidity and imbecility of the Government, who having founded the charge,

charge, dared not advance to the attack. They profited by this want of exertion; and paffing from one extreme rapidly to another, they almoſt unanimouſly took up arms againſt their rulers and oppreſſors. Joined by the French Guards, who, from a long reſidence in the capital, had been peculiarly expoſed to feduction, and who at this deciſive moment abandoned their Sovereign, the Pariſians broke through every obſtacle by which they had hitherto been reſtrained. The ſupplies of arms and ammunition which had been provided for their ſubjugation, were turned againſt the Crown; and the "Hotel des Invalides," the great repoſitory of military ſtores, after a faint reſiſtance, ſurrendered.

The Prince de Lambeſc, who alone, of all the officers commanding the Royal troops in the vicinity of Paris, attempted to carry into execution the plan for difarming the capital, was repulſed in a premature and injudicious attack, which he made at the head of his dragoons, near the entrance of the garden of the Tuilleries. Already the

"Prevot

"Prevot des Marchands," Monſieur de Fleſſelles, convicted of entertaining a correſpondence with the Court, and detected in ſending private intelligence to Monſieur de Launay, Governor of the Baſtile, had been ſeized by the people, and fallen the firſt victim to the general indignation. His head, borne on a lance, exhibited an alarming example of the danger to which adherence to the Sovereign muſt expoſe, in a time of anarchy and inſurrection.

The Baſtile alone remained; and while it continued in the power of the Crown, Paris could not be regarded as free, or even as ſecure from the ſevereſt chaſtiſement. It was inſtantly inveſted by a mixed multitude, compoſed of citizens and ſoldiers who had joined the popular banner. De Launay, who commanded in the caſtle, by an act of perfidy unjuſtifiable under any circumſtances, and which rendered his fate leſs regretted, rather accelerated, than delayed the capture of this important fortreſs. He diſplayed a flag of truce, and demanded a parley; but abuſing the confidence

dence which thefe fignals infpired, he difcharged a heavy fire from the cannon and mufquetry of the place upon the befiegers, and made a confiderable carnage. Far from intimidating, he only augmented, by fo treacherous a breach of faith, the rage of an incenfed populace. They renewed their exertions with a valour raifed to frenzy, and were crowned with fuccefs. The Baftile, that awful engine of defpotifm, whofe name alone diffufed terror, and which for many ages had been facred to filence and defpair, was entered by the victorious affailants. De Launay, feized and dragged to the "Place de Greve," was inftantly difpatched, and his head carried in triumph through the ftreets of Paris.

Few captives, either of inferior or of eminent rank, were found in the apartments of the Baftile. The Count de Lorges, at a very advanced period of life, difcovered in one of the dungeons of the "Tour de la Bertaudiere," was liberated, and exhibited to the public curiofity in the "Palais Royal." His fqualid appearance,

his

his beard which defcended to his waift, and above all, his imbecility, refulting probably from the effect of an imprifonment of thirty-two years, were objects highly calculated to operate upon the fenfes and paffions of every beholder. It is indeed impoffible, however we may lament or condemn the ferocious fpirit which has characterized and difgraced the French revolution, not to participate in the exultation, which a capital and a country fo highly illuminated, and fo long oppreffed, muft have experienced, at the extinction of this deteftable and juftly dreaded prifon of ftate. Nor does the rapidity with which it was captured excite lefs admiration, when its powers of refiftance are confidered, and the fpeedy relief which might have been afforded to it by the numerous bodies of regular forces, with which Paris was furrounded on every fide.

With the Baftile, expired the royal authority and confideration. The defpotifm of the French Princes, which long
prefcription,

prescription, submission, and military strength seemed to render equally sacred and unassailable: which neither the calamities of the close of Louis the Fourteenth's reign, the profligacy and enormities of the succeeding Regency, nor the state of degradation into which the monarchy sunk under Louis the Fifteenth, had ever shaken: that power, which appeared to derive its support almost as much from the loyalty and veneration, as from the dread and terrors of the subject, fell prostrate in the dust, and never betrayed any symptom of returning life.

Paris, liberated from all restraint, or even wholesome police, appeared to riot in the intoxication of freedom; and stained its acquisition by scenes of violence and blood, unworthy the first capital in Europe. Every trace of obedience disappeared; and even the promoters of the late insurrection were not secure from the capricious fury of a frantic and savage populace, who filled the "Place de Greve" with clamours, and frequently tore the victim
whom

whom their indignation had selected, from the hands of justice.

But, at Versailles, consternation and alarm filled the court on the arrival of this extraordinary intelligence. Yielding at once to the united impulse of his terrors and his natural inclinations, the King, without even preserving the forms of Majesty however fallen, repaired to the National Assembly, rather as a suppliant than a monarch. Disordered in his dress, and unaccompanied by his guards or usual attendants, he betrayed his agitation in the speech which he addressed to the States. Only two days preceding this melancholy exhibition of degraded dignity, he had replied to a remonstrance which they presented to him, in terms of determination mixed with menace. He now adopted the language of distress, invoked their assistance, disowned his intention to employ force for the subjection of the capital, assured them that he had already sent orders to withdraw the troops which had invested Paris and Versailles; and professed

feffed his defire to give the moft unequivocal proofs of his deference to the wifhes of his fubjects. He concluded by imploring them to make known thefe his paternal difpofitions, to the inhabitants of the diftracted metropolis.

The Affembly, which trembled a few hours before for its own fafety, and had expected to be offered up as victims to the vengeance of an irritated Sovereign, replied with expreffions of loyalty and affection to thefe gracious declarations, although evidently extorted by fear. It was however far otherwife at Paris, where the populace, deeming their triumph incomplete while the King remained apparently tranquil in his palace; not only exacted his perfonal and immediate prefence among them, to fanction their outrages on his authority; but accompanied this demand with menaces, if refufed, of fetting fire to Verfailles, and at once extinguifhing the obnoxious Princes of the Houfe of Bourbon in the flames. Perhaps a monarch endowed with qualities

ties such as Louis the Fourteenth possessed, would perhaps have refused compliance with this humiliating requisition; and while his army was yet entire, and the royal dignity not totally degraded, have embraced the generous resolution of meeting the storm, of trying the fortune of war, and at least devolving to his successor the prerogatives, which at his accession he had received and exercised. But Louis the Sixteenth possessed no abilities competent to so magnanimous and unequal a struggle. He had already abandoned his attempts to maintain the Royal power in its original vigour; and he had now scarcely any option between the loss of his throne, and a complete submission to the arbitrary pleasure of a populace, thirsting for blood, inflamed by success, and daily offering up victims to its revenge.

Under these melancholy circumstances, He did not hesitate to yield obedience to the mandate, which it was no longer safe to refuse. After such a night as Charles the First may be supposed to have passed, previous to his ascending the scaffold; but unattended with that serenity and fortitude, which eminently distinguished the English Monarch in the last act of life, he set out for Paris. Conscious however, of the peril attendant on his appearance in the metropolis of his dominions, and doubtful of escaping from the rage of the multitude to whom he was to be presented, he prepared for death, as at least, a possible event. He received the sacrament, made some private dispositions of affairs, and gave various orders in consequence. Though desirous to see and embrace his son and daughter before his departure, he yet had firmness sufficient to refuse himself this indulgence, as fearing that it might too deeply affect, and disqualify him for the part which he was to perform. " J'en aurai plus de plaisir," said he, " si je reviens." A gentleman who was near his person on this occasion, encouraging him, and venturing to answer

for

for his safety, the King replied, "Henry Quatre valoit mieux que moi; et cependant on l'a affassiné."

Though he quitted Versailles at an early hour, it was late before he entered Paris, from the immense multitudes who assembled to see him pass, and who testified no sentiments of loyalty in their acclamations. When arrived at the "Place de Greve," and conducted to the "Hotel de Ville," the new Mayor, Monsieur Bailli, who had been elected to supply the late unfortunate first magistrate, insulted the fallen Prince by a mock surrender of the keys of his capital; which he accompanied with a sarcastic and insolent reflexion on the different situation in which Henry the Fourth stood, when he received a similar testimony of its submission and allegiance. The cries of the people, who insisted that the King should shew himself on the balcony, compelled him to give this last proof of his deference to their wishes; and to add to the condescension, he accepted from the hands of the Mayor, the National cockade, which he firſt carried to his lips, and then placed in his hat. After having been detained and exhibited as a captive to his own ſubjects during the greater part of the day, without ſuſtenance or refreſhment of any kind, he was at length permitted to return to Verſailles, and to conceal his emotions in the privacy of his own apartments.

While this humiliating ſcene was acting before the eyes of all France, which were turned towards ſo unuſual and attractive a ſight, the adherents to the late meaſures, terrified at the menaces thrown out againſt them, and dreading the moſt fatal conſequences of popular fury, profited of the King's abſence and viſit to his capital, to effect their own eſcape.

The Count d'Artois, regarding himſelf as peculiarly marked out for proſcription and impeachment, and apprehenſive that even his proximity of blood to the Sovereign might prove an inſufficient protection to his life, fled among the firſt, carrying with him his ſons, the Dukes d'An-gouleme

gouleme and de Berri; two youths who were succeſſively preſumptive heirs to the Crown, in caſe of the demiſe of the Dauphin. In the hurry of a precipitate retreat, it was found extremely difficult to furniſh a few hundred louis d'ors to a Prince, for whoſe expenſive gratifications, only ſome days before, the treaſures of the monarchy were inſufficient. He took the road to Flanders; and was already far advanced towards the frontiers, before his departure was known or ſuſpected at Paris. When ſo diſtinguiſhed a perſonage, and one ſo nearly allied to the throne, deemed himſelf no longer ſafe even in the Royal reſidence, it cannot excite wonder that thoſe of a leſs elevated condition, and who were equally obnoxious to an enraged populace, ſhould conſult their ſafety by inſtant flight. The principal roads were covered with illuſtrious fugitives, under every poſſible diſguiſe and concealment. The Prince of Condé quitted Chantilly, followed by his ſon and grandſon, the Dukes of Bourbon and Enghien. The Prince of Conti, the

laſt

last in succession of the Blood Royal, after undergoing many extremities of hunger and fatigue, arrived at Luxembourg; to which place likewise the Marechal de Broglio, abandoning his army, repaired without delay.

The Duchess of Polignac, so long unrival'd in the affections of the Queen, and round whom all the pleasures of the Court of Versailles were used to assemble; tearing herself from this scene of dissipation, attain'd with difficulty the city of Bale in Switzerland; after having encountered numerous dangers, and been preserved from the last degree of violence as she passed through Sens, by the happy presence of mind which distinguished an Abbé, by whom she was accompanied. At Bale, by one of those singular accidents which evince the power of fortune, she found in the inn at which she alighted, the late Minister, Neckar; who having passed through Swabia after his dismission, on his way to Geneva, here first received from his enemies, the intel-

intelligence of the revolution. The Baron de Breteuil, purfued by the moft marked deteftation of his countrymen, evaded, as well as the Prince de Lambefc, the fnares prepared to intercept them: the former reaching Bern in fafety, as the latter did Turin. Monfieur de Befenval, lefs fortunate, was feized at Brie Comte Robert; and even the folicitations of Neckar himfelf, who endeavoured to interpofe in his behalf, were infufficient to obtain his enlargement.

In this general confternation, the Queen, abandoned by all her deareft connexions, remained with her two children, friendlefs, and almoft alone, in the palace of Verfailles. No Prince of the Royal Family ventured to abide the ftorm, except the Count de Provence; who during the continuance of all thefe diforders, had enjoyed a diftinguifhed fhare, at leaft of negative approbation; and whofe conduct throughout the critical circumftances which preceded the fedition of Paris, had been fuch

as

as to conciliate, in some degree, the popular favour.

The Duke of Orleans, to whose intrigues, or opposition to the Crown, may be greatly ascribed the rapid progress of the general discontent, and the excesses of the people; viewed from the " Palais Royal" with secret pleasure, the effects of his machinations, and enjoyed his triumph over the vanquished court. The military command of the National troops, and of the capital, were conferred by almost unanimous delegation on the Marquis de la Fayette; as the supreme civil and municipal jurisdiction devolved on Bailli, Mayor of Paris. The union of both these powers, was however frequently found unequal to imposing proper restraints upon the ungoverned passions and savage violence of a populace, new to freedom, and who stained its acquisition by daily acts of vengeance and cruelty. The heads of Foulon and Berthier, one of whom had occupied a high situation in the
late

late miniftry, and the other had been intendant of Paris, were carried through the ftreets; and the circumftances with which the death of thefe eminent perfons were accompanied, are only to be compared in horror and atrocity with thofe attendant on the maffacre of St. Bartholomew, or the affaffination of the Marechal d'Ancre under Louis the Thirteenth.

Meanwhile, at the inftigation and requeft of the National Affembly, Neckar was recalled, and invited by letters of the moft flattering, and even penitential tenor, from the King himfelf, to refume the fuperintendance of the finances. He yielded, though with apparent reluctance, to thefe entreaties; and repaired to Court, loaded with expreffions of general attachment and veneration in every place through which he paffed: while the credulous and deluded multitude expected from his prefence, a fpeedy redrefs of all their grievances, the revival of public credit, and a remedy to the fcarcity of grain, which had excited the clamours of the capital and the kingdom. To the admiration and astonishment of mankind, in an absolute monarchy so strongly cemented as that of France appeared to have been, and in which loyalty was antiently esteemed to be characteristic of every class of citizens, no efforts were made to support the Royal power. An enthusiastic passion for liberty pervaded all the provinces; and the revolution, commenced on the banks of the Seine, spread with equal rapidity and unanimity, to the foot of the Alps and Pyrenees; to the Rhine and the Mediterranean.

No permanent calm succeeded to this storm of popular indignation. Elated with the possession of freedom, and exercising in many instances, a tyranny more oppressive and severe than that from which they had just escaped, the people meditated new and greater invasions on the dignity, as well as the prerogatives of the Crown. The press, freed even from that wholesome and necessary restriction, which Governments the most relaxed impose upon the publication of opinions, compensated for the fetters which

it

it had so long worn, by giving birth to every species of licentious production and insolent attack upon persons of the highest rank. The Queen was peculiarly the object of these libellous invectives; and every accusation private or political, which malignity could invent, to alienate the affections and irritate the passions of mankind against her, was circulated, and publicly exposed to sale. Although all the pomp and majesty, which in better times had surrounded and concealed the Sovereign, was now entirely withdrawn: though only guarded by the burgesses of Versailles, and destitute of any military protection against insult and outrage, Louis the Sixteenth stood exposed to every enterprize which a mutinous capital might undertake or execute; yet some vestiges of personal liberty he still retained. He was free to enjoy the diversion of the chace; and the National Assembly, convoked at Versailles, continued to hold its meetings there, under his immediate superintendance and inspection. It was even thought decent and necessary, on the part of the new tribunes of the people, to march some regiments, in the month of September, on whose adherence they conceived that they could safely rely, to perform the ordinary functions of state; at the same time that they prevented any escape, if such was intended by the King.

But, where so many inflammable materials were collected, it was not possible that any considerable time could elapse before they burst into a conflagration. After one or two attempts, which the vigilance and activity of La Fayette prevented from being carried into full execution, the populace of Paris, excited by various arts, and incensed at the Queen for having brought the Dauphin, and presented him to the officers of the regular troops after a public entertainment, rose as by universal consent, and determined to march to Versailles. By what motives, or with what intentions, the conductors of this armed mob were actuated, it is perhaps impossible at present positively to assert. The deepest and blackest designs have, by popular malignity, been attributed to the

Duke

Duke of Orleans; no less than the attainment of the Regency, at whatever price, and by every mode, however treasonable or flagitious. Many of the circumstances which distinguished that extraordinary scene, unquestionably evince a plan not more artful than nefarious; and which seemed calculated, by operating on the fears of the Sovereign, to induce him to abandon the throne, and seek his safety in flight; while the Queen, who was more an object of national obloquy and aversion, might be instantly offered up as a victim to the frantic multitude.

It is difficult to do justice to the horrors of a night, similar only to those which are furnished by the annals of Charles the Ninth, and which reminds us of the times of Catherine of Medicis. Posterity will scarcely credit, that at the conclusion of the eighteenth century, and in a country eminently distinguished by all the softer virtues of humanity, acts of blood and ferocity more savage than the Janizaries of Constantinople usually exercise

against

against their despots, were performed with impunity. The singularity and incredibility of the recital will be augmented by recollecting, that many of the most violent among these ruffians, were women; or, at least habited in a female dress. Armed with every destructive weapon, they assaulted the guards who were stationed at the door of the Queen's apartments, burst into them, murdered those who opposed their progress, and penetrated to the chamber in which she slept. The efforts which were made to retard their fury, and the cries of "Sauvez la Reine," which echoed through the palace, gave her an instant in which to escape. The first Queen in Europe was saved from a death the most ignominious, by the interval of almost a single moment. Undressed, and nearly naked, she gained a private staircase, which conveyed her to the King, who received her in his arms, where she fell senseless with terror. The materials of the bed from which she had just risen, after undergoing the strictest search, in hopes of discovering the unhappy object of their pursuit,

suit, were scattered over the room, as some gratification to their disappointed vengeance.

Louis the Sixteenth himself, appearing on the balcony of his apartment, in the language and attitude of supplication, vainly implored the populace to spare his guards, whom he saw massacred at his feet, without the power of extending to them any relief. He as vainly besought the Queen to yield to the necessity of the time, and to retire to Rambouillet, where her person would at least be secure. Exerting a courage superior to her sex, and elevated above a sense of the danger to which she was so conspicuously exposed, she firmly persisted in her refusal to fly; and declared her determination to accompany the King, and at least to expire as she had lived, a Queen of France. Yet, conscious of the probability of her falling a sacrifice to the popular rage, she armed herself with a poniard, as a last resource against the degradation of plebeian violence and brutality.

It is impossible, how much soever we may condemn

condemn certain parts of her conduct and character, not to admire the heroifm and magnanimity of this deportment, in which we feem to recognize the blood of fo many Emperors from whom fhe defcended. The weaknefs of the woman was notwithftanding, mingled with the fortitude of the Sovereign; and when fhe entered the coach which was to convey herfelf and the captive King from Verfailles to Paris, terrified at the cries of a furious multitude who feemed to demand her forfeit life, fhe threw herfelf into the arms of La Fayette, who offered her his hand at the door of the carriage; and whofe protection fhe invoked to preferve her from outrage and death. Placing the Dauphin in her lap, and feated by her hufband, the cavalcade moved flowly towards the capital; while the heads of the murdered "Gardes du Corps," borne on poles, and held up to her view, prefented a melancholy profpect of her own probable deftiny. They at length reached the palace of the Thuilleries, thus accompanied, and took poffeffion of that

that part of it destined for their reception and residence: while cannon, mounted at the principal avenues, under pretence of safety and defence, secured them from rescue, and rendered escape impracticable.

Perhaps no day so ignominious to the Royal dignity had been beheld, since the elevation of the Capetian Princes to the throne of France. The capture and imprisonment of Louis the Ninth at Damietta, of King John at Poictiers, and of Francis the First at the battle of Pavia, however unfortunate and humiliating, yet were at last softened by many considerations. Those Monarchs were all taken in arms, after exerting the most heroic acts of valour against their conquerors, and owed their misfortunes only to the chance of war. Even Henry the Third, when he fled from his capital, pursued by the Guises, yet retained his personal independence, and soon returned to besiege and to chastise his rebellious subjects. Louis the Sixteenth, sunk below esteem or commiseration, and not having exerted either ability

lity or courage in the defence of his invaded prerogatives, only held a precarious life at the mercy of a seditious and insolent populace, who having already imprisoned, might in any moment of resentment, terminate the reign of their fallen and degraded King. The palace in which he was confined, having been in a great measure neglected for more than a century, during which time Paris had rarely seen any Sovereign resident in the metropolis, was totally unfit for the reception of a Court; and even the apartments which were occupied by the King himself, were in so ruinous or decayed a condition, as not altogether to exclude the inclemency of the weather. To this situation was a Monarch reduced, who only a few months before, might be regarded as at the summit of human greatness; and the foundations of whose throne, strengthened by long possession and by habits of obedience, seemed to bid defiance to all the ordinary convulsions which overturn empires, and destroy the firmest fabrics of human power and wisdom.

While

While thefe fcenes of outrage and violence were exhibiting in France, it is difficult to imagine a picture of more complete ferenity than England prefented; and this internal repofe was accompanied with every circumftance of external profperity, and augmenting national confideration. The year which immediately fucceeded the malady of George the Third, may be ranked among the happieft of his reign, whether it be confidered as perfonally affecting himfelf, or as productive of felicity to his people. The recent danger from which he had efcaped, rendered his health and fafety peculiarly precious to his fubjects; as the animated expreffions of their attachment and loyalty muft have deeply touched the heart of a Prince, infinitely fenfible to thefe genuine marks of affection. The character of the Sovereign was not more formed to produce, than that of his Adminiftration was to perpetuate the general tranquillity. The conduct of Mr. Pitt during the whole progrefs of the late commotions in France, may be held up as a model of political honor and rectitude; perhaps, equally so of wisdom. Unlike to Richlieu, who fomented the causes of discord between Charles the First, and his Parliament: unlike to Vergennes, who stimulated the Americans to resistance; and after a series of indirect and insidious arts, violated the most solemn treaties in order to assure their final independence: the English Minister steadily and systematically adhered to the most exact neutrality. The native elevation of his mind, and the magnanimity which has ever characterised his measures, rendered him incapable of descending to the little artifices of crooked and vulgar statesmen. The probity of his private life pervaded and marked his public line of action; nor did so uncommon and dignified a mode of proceeding, under circumstances which might seem to justify and authorize a more relaxed conduct, fail to produce its full effect on the two nations who were peculiarly affected by it, as well as on the other states of Europe. Some approbation, if not admiration, is indeed due

due to a Government, who have been able to unite vigour, energy, and protection, with the most religious adherence to the national faith, and to every principle of sound and generous policy.

The period which is comprised between the months of May 1789 and 1790, like the reign of Antoninus Pius, affords few materials for history, drawn from the interior events of the time. England, at peace with all the world, in the bosom of repose, saw her commerce and manufactures expand, her credit augment, and her name excite respect among the most distant nations; while many of the great surrounding European kingdoms were either involved in foreign war, or desolated by domestic troubles. This tranquillity was not however allied to an ignominious and enervate sloth; but, on the contrary, was secured by vigilance, activity, and exertion. In conjunction with Prussia and Holland, Great Britain indirectly extended her attention and succour to Gustavus the Third, sinking under an unequal contest with the vast empire of Russia.

Ruffia. She reftrained and arrefted Denmark, even after that power, as an auxiliary of the Court of Peterfburgh, had already taken up arms, and committed hoftilities againft Sweden. She fignified to Leopold, who had recently fucceeded to the thrones of Hungary and Bohemia, her defire that he would recall his troops from the Banks of the Danube; and fhe fuftained by her negociations the firmnefs of the Ottoman counfels, while fhe filently, but not lefs decidedly, impofed limits on the ambition of their great enemy Catherine the Second, by prohibiting her fleet from prefuming to quit the Baltic, and to complete the deftruction of the Turks in the Archipelago.

In this exalted fituation, to which perhaps no parallel in our annals can be adduced, fince the termination of the fhort, but fplendid protectorate of Cromwell, a ftorm unexpectedly and fuddenly arofe from a quarter, where it would feem, that no forefight or precautions could have anticipated the danger. Among the new and unexplored paths of commerce, which the

fpirit

spirit of a discerning and adventurous people had attempted to open since the peace of 1783, were particularly two, which appeared to promise the most beneficial returns. The first was a whale fishery, similar to that which had been carried on for ages near the coasts of Greenland; but transferred to the Southern hemisphere, near the extremity of Patagonia, and in the stormy seas which surround Cape Horn; as well as in the Pacific Ocean. In the course of a few years, this branch of trade had augmented rapidly, and was found on trial to afford very important advantages; nor had it received any impediment from the vague pretensions of the Spanish Crown to the sovereignty of the shores washed by that ocean, which was the scene of their exertions.

The second of these enterprizes, original in its own nature, able in its conception, bold in its execution, and having no precedent for its guidance, was directed to countries and to objects almost as much unknown to geographical, as to commercial knowledge

ledge or experience. It demanded many qualities rarely and difficultly combined: a confiderable capital; minifterial approbation; faithful and capable conductors; dextrous navigators; and above all, much time and perfeverance to ripen, and ultimately recompenfe the perfons engaging in fo eccentric and expenfive an expedition. This extraordinary union of talents and circumftances was, however, found in men of no fuperior defcription among the mercantile inhabitants of London; and it will remain a ftriking monument to future ages, of the energy, capacity, and nautical ability, which diftinguifh the prefent century and the Britifh nation, above the moft enlightened periods of any antient or modern people.

The North Weft coaft of America, the part of the earth to which this embarkation was deftined, was not only fo remote, but fo undefined, if I may be allowed the expreffion, that its very exiftence remained unknown or doubtful, before the difcoveries of the reign of George the Third.

In

At the commencement of the present century, it was thought to be almost as much beyond the ordinary bounds of navigation, as the islands of the Hesperides appeared to the Greeks; and Swift himself, only eighty years ago, when he composed the entertaining voyages of Lemuel Gulliver, esteeming it the proper region of fable and romance, selected it for the position of his imaginary Brobdignag. The immense tract of land, extending northward from California and New Albion to the Frozen Sea, had, indeed, in a more recent period, been partly explored, and faintly traced by Cook; though much remained for future enterprize and industry to accomplish, before this discovery could be converted to any purpose of public utility. He had, however, ascertained the existence of the continent; and he had received from the barbarous natives, with whom he established a species of barter, some valuable specimens of furs, in exchange for European commodities of a far inferior nature.

The hope of procuring a confiderable number of thefe rare and coftly fkins, for the fale of which a very advantageous market prefented itfelf at Canton in China, was the leading inducement to the adventurers, who engaged in the expedition. But, in the purfuit of private emolument, objects of general and national confequence were necessarily implicated and interwoven. Behind this coaft, to the eaftward, lay the vaft continent of America; opening a field to commercial activity and refearch, in which the imagination itfelf was loft. The difcovery of a communication through this unexplored country, and which may ultimately connect it, to a certain degree, with our fettlements in Hudfon's Bay, appears from their account, not to be totally vifionary, though it was regarded as fuch by Cook himfelf.

Conceptions and enterprizes more calculated to enlarge the fphere of induftry; to connect the moft remote parts of the planet of the earth by the bands of amity and commerce; to extend the limits

of

of the human mind; and to immortalize, while they enriched the nation which originated them, have perhaps scarcely ever been imagined or executed. They were not inferior to the moſt ſublime and daring expeditions of antient Greece, and ſeemed to partake of the ſpirit of Columbus: though the preſent age, familiarized to naval ſkill and enterprize, no longer ſees with the ſame admiration, or confers the ſame eulogiums on modern candidates for fame; who are ſeldom regarded through any other medium than that of utility, or pecuniary advantage.

Animated by theſe views, and having received the moſt affirmative marks of the protection of Government previous to their departure, five ſhips were fitted out from London in 1785, and the two ſucceeding years. Four of theſe veſſels, after doubling Cape Horn, arrived ſafely on the North Weſt coaſt of America. The ſanguine expectations which had been entertained, of effecting a lucrative exchange of commodities with the natives, were fully and speedily realized. Cargoes of the finest furs were procured, and sold to the Chinese, even under great commercial discouragements and pecuniary impositions, at so high a price, as amply to reimburse and enrich the adventurers. Other attempts, of a similar nature, were made from Bengal; and two vessels were successively dispatched from the Ganges to the same coast, in the year 1786. A factory was established at Nootka Sound, a port situated in the fiftieth degree of northern latitude, on the shore of America. Possession of it was solemnly taken in the name of the Sovereign and Crown of England: amicable treaties were concluded with the chiefs of the neighbouring districts; and a tract of land was purchased from one of them, on which the new proprietors proceeded to form a settlement, and to construct storehouses. Every thing bore the appearance of a rising colony, and each year opened new sources of commerce and advantage.

Although

Although individuals, occupied in exertions of this private nature, could not be expected to extend their views or efforts to objects of public utility, yet some further information was collaterally and incidentally acquired, respecting the continent of America, in the course of their voyages. It is even pretended that a sloop, named the "Washington," navigated for some hundred miles along a vast number of islands, scattered in a sea, which intersects that continent in a north-east direction; and though the accounts hitherto received or transmitted, of this extraordinary and interesting fact, are not either so minute, or so accurate, as by any means to entitle them to be implicitly received, yet they appear to be not totally destitute of foundation, or probability. Every prospect, either of national advantage, or of private emolument, which the commerce of these coasts seemed to promise to Great Britain, was, however, destined to experience a sudden and unexpected suspension.

On

On the 6th of May, 1789, two Spanish ships of war entered Nootka Sound; the commanding officer of which, after making every profession of amity during several days, seized on the English vessels, in the name of his Sovereign, as they successively arrived from various parts of the coast, imprisoned the crews, confiscated or plundered the cargoes, and ultimately carried them as lawful prizes to St. Blas, in Mexico. Violations so unprovoked, not only of the peace subsisting between the two Monarchies, but of all the laws established between civilized nations, were accompanied and aggravated by every circumstance of duplicity, insolence, and cruelty; while they were contrasted with the most friendly assistance and attentions, shewn to the captains of two American ships, the "Washington" and the "Columbia;" who had been brought by the same commercial inducements to the port of Nootka. These testimonies of protection and regard were even carried so far by the Spaniards, as to compel the crew of one of the captured

English

English vessels to assist in navigating the "Columbia" to Canton; through which channel, the first regular and authentic account of these acts of hostility, was officially transmitted to the English Administration, though they had been preceded by some vague and indistinct intimations of the same nature, made by the Spanish embassador at the Court of London.

The conduct of the First Minister on receiving this intelligence, evinced no less the magnanimity than the decision of his character. Without descending to the tedious and humiliating forms of request with the Court of Spain, which might elude and protract, if not ultimately refuse, according to its usual policy, any reparation for these outrages; he, in the first instance, by a message from the King, informed the two Houses of Parliament of the whole series of transactions. He clearly evinced the nullity and injustice of any general pretensions on the part of the Spanish Crown, to a territory, discovered, planted, and occupied by the English; but in particular, to the Port of Nootka,

situated

situated at a distance from any known settlement belonging to that nation. He professed his anxious desire to terminate by amicable explanation and treaty, the present cause of dispute. He at the same time declared his determined intention, not only to exact from the Court of Madrid an adequate satisfaction and compensation for the injuries recently sustained; but to compel Spain to renounce decidedly and formally, any indefinite claim which she might have set up, either to the exclusive navigation of the Pacific ocean, or to the sovereignty of the whole North West coast of America. He called on the loyalty, dignity, and honour of the House of Commons for support, in maintaining these invaded rights by force of arms, if Spain should be insensible to the language of reason.

The approbation which so manly an appeal to the nation excited, was general and animated. The leaders of Opposition joined in that sentiment, and expressed their conviction of the wisdom as well as necessity

necessity of sustaining by every military and naval exertion, the effect of negotiation. The celerity with which these resolutions were followed, in the equipment of a powerful armament, was calculated to augment the high reputation of the Ministry throughout Europe, while it called into action all the resources of the kingdom. A dissolution of Parliament, unquestionably judicious under the circumstance of a probably impending war, followed these demonstrations of resentment, and demands of reparation.

If we compare the energy and decision of so vigorous a line of conduct, with that which was adopted by Sir Robert Walpole or Lord North, in similar situations, the contrast must be highly flattering to the present Administration. The sluggish and reluctant disinclination of the former, to perceive or to resent the depredations committed by the Spaniards upon the English trade, during a long series of years; while it emboldened the

Y enemy,

enemy, depreffed the genius of England: until Parliament, roufed by fuch a continuation of infults and indignities, at length vindicated the national honour, and drove the Minifter from the fuperintendance of affairs.

The temporifing and pufillanimous counfels of Lord North, in the difpute refpecting the Falkland iflands; and the ultimate termination of it, which left the right undecided, and even afferted by the Court of Madrid, at the fame moment that from motives of political convenience, Spain thought proper to cede the contefted territory to England: thefe humiliating meafures, expofed and reprobated by the pen of Junius, ftand in need of no comment, and are fufficiently appreciated by a juft and difcerning people.

Spain was no longer governed by Charles the Third, at the time when thefe interefting events took place. That Prince, after a reign of above twenty years as Sovereign of Naples,

had

had ascended the Spanish throne on the death of his brother Ferdinand the Sixth, in 1759; and expired at a very advanced period of life, in December, 1788. His unconcealed dislike of the English nation, from whom in his youth he had received some signal benefits, as well as some painful and personal humiliations, had probably induced him, even more than the ties of blood, or connexions of policy with the Court of France, to join that kingdom in two successive wars which she carried on against Great Britain.

To the counsels of his reign, and probably to a systematic plan in concert with the Cabinet of Versailles, for attacking the commerce, and setting limits to the enterprizes of England on the North West coast of America, we may without injustice attribute the acts of violence, committed by Don Martinez in the Port of Nootka. The short period, comprising scarcely five months, which elapsed between the death of Charles the Third, and those infractions of the peace previously subsisting between the two Crowns, leave no room to doubt that the original orders were issued during the life of the late Sovereign.

Charles the Fourth succeeded to the Spanish monarchy under these circumstances. Though of a mature age, his character was little known or understood beyond the limits of his own dominions. In the early part of his life he had appeared to evince sentiments more Castilian, than any of the descendants of Philip the Fifth had hitherto discovered; and to promise a reign, in which the feelings of a common origin and descent would influence less on affairs of state, than a wise consideration of the true policy and interests, becoming a genuine King of Spain. It may however be questioned, whether this anticipation of his maxims and supposed line of conduct, will be confirmed by experience; and whether he will emancipate himself from the partialities, naturally connected with his near affinity to Louis the Sixteenth. The same Ministers seem to govern, and the same principles to animate

mate the Court of Madrid, which have uniformly characterized it since the extinction of the Spanish branch of the House of Austria: and the time is probably still distant, when the pernicious effects of the treaty of Utrecht in uniting two monarchies, which for ages anterior to that event had never acted in conjunction against Great Britain, will have finally ceased to operate.

Meanwhile, the efforts of the First Minister to terminate the present dispute by negotiation, kept equal pace with the exertions made to equip a formidable naval force. At the same time that a fleet, the command of which was destined to Lord Howe, assembled at Portsmouth, Mr. Fitzherbert was dispatched as ambassador to Madrid, in order to try the effect of remonstrance and expostulation. The English people, unanimous in their approbation of the measures pursued, and in their demand of reparation for the injuries sustained, loudly called for instant war, or for the most unequivocal and satisfactory concessions.

The

The convulsions and embarrassed state of the French monarchy, together with the personal situation of the King of France, appeared to render an adherence to, or completion of the family compact impracticable, however well inclined the Court of Versailles might be supposed, to assist and support her ally.

Spain doubtless felt and regretted this incapacity, which compelled her to commence a war against England, unassisted by any European power; and the event of which, in the present circumstances, might be fatal to her grandeur or commerce in every part of the world. She seemed to yield to these obvious considerations; and the Spanish Ministry towards the close of July, agreed to make a compensation for the losses, sustained by the English adventurers plundered at Nootka, as a basis or preliminary to a final and amicable arrangement. Notwithstanding, however, this apparent desire of adjusting the points in dispute, and of avoiding the ultimate appeal to the sword, every exertion was not only made

in

in the ports of Cadiz and Ferrol, to fit out a numerous fquadron; but the Spanifh ambaffador at the Court of France, expended the treafures of his mafter, in endeavours to induce the National Affembly to adopt the quarrels of Charles the Fourth, and to fulfil in its whole extent the obligations of the family compact. His labours, though not equally fuccefsful, as, under more propitious circumftances they might have proved, yet produced a vote favourable to the views and wifhes of the Crown of Spain. A general profeffion on the part of the National Affembly, of adherence to the ftipulations formed between the two nations; and a refolution inftantly to arm a confiderable naval force at Breft, were procured and publifhed. The hopes of a fpeedy and permanent accommodation between the Courts of London and Madrid, which the firft conceffion on the part of the latter power had excited, gradually grew more uncertain and problematical. Autumn advanced, without any certainty or decifion on this great point; and though the

the fleet of England, which had cruized in the Bay of Bifcay during near fix weeks, returned again to Spithead, without having feen an enemy, yet the expectation of an eventual rupture was rather augmented than diminifhed.

While thefe negociations and armaments detained the Weft of Europe in fufpenfe, the moft important and unexpected events had taken place among the Princes of the Germanic empire, in confequence of the death of the late Emperor Jofeph the Second. That reftlefs and turbulent Prince, exhaufted in body, and agitated in mind, expired at Vienna in the commencement of the prefent year. His vaft, but divided and revolted provinces, devolved to his brother Leopold, Great Duke of Tufcany. Few Sovereigns have ever acceded to a throne under more critical and alarming circumftances. Though Laudohn had clofed his brilliant career of military glory, and even fhed a luftre over the laft years of Jofeph, by the capture of Belgrade: though the Turks had been driven beyond the Danube, and the Imperial troops had at length penetrated into Servia and Moldavia; yet thefe advantages, bought with three campaigns, and preceded by defeats and difafters, offered a very inadequate compenfation for the calamities, which menaced or afflicted every other part of the dominions of the Houfe of Auftria. Hungary, fo renowned for its enthufiaftic loyalty and attachment to Maria Therefa, when that Princefs was involved in the deepeft diftrefs, had been alienated by her fucceffor; who infulted their moft facred prejudices, while he invaded their moft valuable immunities. Pofterity will fcarcely believe that this injudicious and infatuated Prince, foon after his acceffion, from refentment to the Hungarians, not only removed the crown and regalia of that monarchy from Buda, the antient capital, to Vienna: but, as a mark of fcorn and contempt, caufed thefe venerable infignia of the kingly dignity, inexpreffibly precious in the eftimation of the people, to be conveyed from one capital

tal to the other, in the common ſtage waggon.

The King of Pruſſia hung over Bohemia, with a prodigious army, ready to enter that kingdom. The German Princes were almoſt univerſally diſaffected to the late Emperor, and had reprobated his inſidious projects for an exchange of territory with the Elector Palatine. The Netherlands, irritated by a long ſeries of oppreſſion, confiſcation, and violation of all their antient liberties, had renounced any allegiance to a Prince, whom they regarded not as a protector, but a tyrant. Philip the Second, when he recalled the ſanguinary Duke of Alva, was ſcarcely more deteſted, and had not more completely loſt the low countries, than Joſeph the Second had done. Dalton, though at the head of a regular and formidable body of forces, had been compelled precipitately to evacuate Bruſſels, and to ſeek his ſafety in a diſorderly and ignominious retreat. Luxembourg alone remained, of all the ten provinces, when Leopold
ſucceeded

succeeded to his brother; and Flanders no longer even listened to the propositions of accommodation, which Joseph in his dying moments offered to his revolted subjects.

In this situation, surrounded with difficulties occasioned by the ambition and despotism of his predecessor, the new King of Hungary, after some months of delay and irresolution, wisely yielded to the necessity, imposed on him by the distracted condition of his affairs. The Courts of Berlin and of London, acting in concert, and sustained by a Prussian army, gave law to the House of Austria. Leopold consented to abandon the alliance of the Empress of Russia; to restore to Turkey the territories lately acquired; and to receive his Flemish subjects into favour, after conceding and confirming, in the most extended degree, all their liberties and privileges. This vigorous and successful interposition was instantly followed by a peremptory requisition, on the part of the same Powers to Catherine the Second, by which that haughty and enterprizing

Princess was required to follow the example exhibited by the King of Hungary; and to grant an equitable peace to the Ottoman Porte, as well as to conclude the war which she carried on against Sweden.

From so humiliating a necessity, the Empress extricated herself by one of the most rapid, unforeseen, and perhaps masterly strokes of policy, which is to be found in the annals of the present century. She made a peace with that King of Sweden, against whom she had not scrupled, a few years since, to excite his own soldiers and subjects to revolt: who had scarcely escaped from captivity at Wybourg, by forcing a passage through the Russian fleet, with which he was surrounded: and who had not only committed hostilities and waged war upon her empire; but was supposed to have drawn his pen against her reputation, and to have accused her to Europe, and to future times, as an usurper, insatiable in her thirst of power, and destitute of faith or honour. Only a few days intervened between the most

rancorous

rancorous difplay of perfonal enmity, and the folemn exchange of the ratifications of peace: while Catherine, liberated by this fuccefsful exertion from an enemy who detained her fleet in the Baltic, and who might prefent himfelf at the very gates of her capital, affumed new vigour, difdained to fubmit to the mandates of Pruffia, and continued her military operations againft the Turks.

She did not ftop here; but, irritated by the attempt to fetter her arms and limit her conquefts, fhe preffed Guftavus the Third to enter into a confederacy againft thofe powers, with whom he had been fo lately in ftrict alliance; and to whofe timely interference or good offices, he had been in a great meafure indebted for his prefervation. She negociated anew with the Prince Regent and Cabinet of Denmark, whom the interpofition of England had hitherto reluctantly retained in neutrality. She corrupted, or perfuaded the Polifh Diet to exprefs fentiments hoftile to Pruffia; and encouraged Spain to refufe refuse compliance with the demands of the British Government.

Under these circumstances and appearances, hostile or inauspicious to the repose of Europe, the month of October commenced. During its progress, the hopes and fears of the nation were painfully suspended, by the uncertainty of the final event. The impatience and anxiety, natural to, and inseparable from such a situation, were infinitely augmented by the secrecy and silence, which surrounded and concealed the operations of the cabinet. The powers and energies of Government, concentered round the First Minister, and vested in his person, exhibited to the English nation, all the vigor, celerity, and decision of a despotism, unaccompanied with its characteristic and concomitant evils. Though the finest and most numerous fleet which Great Britain had ever equipped, lay at Spithead, ready to stand out into the Atlantic upon the shortest notice: though Admiral Cornish, at the head of eight ships of the line, had already set

sail;

sail; and, favored by an easterly wind, was clear of the Channel: though a detachment of the Guards, to the number of above two thousand men, were under orders to march to Portsmouth; and every preparation was made to facilitate their prompt embarkation: though the blow which impended over the Spanish monarchy, hung by a single thread, and might every instant fall; yet, not a whisper transpired, to gratify the curiosity of an eager capital, and an expecting country.

Universal ignorance, or fanciful conjecture prevailed, respecting the destination of these powerful naval and military armaments; while the magnitude and scattered position of the Spanish dominions, from the mouth of the Mississippi to that of the river Plate, left an ample field for the imagination, and afforded scope for unbounded assertion. To those who recollected the delays, the publicity, and the timidity which degraded the counsels, and frustrated the measures

or

or exertions of England, during the Administration which conducted the American war, the present contrast was matter of equal wonder and admiration. The nation, conscious that its honour and its interests were committed to a a depositary of transcendent integrity and firmness, patiently waited the winding up of the catastrophe, with eyes fixed on its conductor. Opinion fluctuated rapidly and capriciously from war to peace, as the most trifling events appeared to indicate the one or the other; and October expired as it had begun, in uncertainty and suspence.

During the three first days of the succeeding month, as every hour might be supposed to decide on this momentous question, expectation seemed to have attained its highest point; while the rapid approach of that period, when Parliament was summoned to meet for the dispatch of public business, and the advanced season of the year, superadded to the length of time which had already elapsed since

the

the commencement of the negotiation, appeared to preclude the poſſibility of any further delay. It was not till the fourth of November, a day already rendered memorable and auſpicious in the annals of Great Britain, that the meſſenger ſo long expected, arrived with pacific intelligence. Spain, after a reſiſtance proportioned to the magnitude and importance of the objects conteſted, and after peremptory and reiterated refuſals to concede upon points, equally affecting her pride and her intereſts; relaxed at once from this tone, complied with the demands of England, and ſigned a " Convention," which terminated every paſt or preſent cauſe of diſpute between the two Crowns.

To the wiſdom and moderation of the Spaniſh Firſt Miniſter, the Count de Florida Blanca, this timely and temperate reſolution, which arreſted the ſword already unſheathed, was attributed, by an opinion, not only general, but unqueſtionably ſuſtained on high authority and evidence.

evidence. If the historian was permitted to speculate upon the events of futurity; or if, from ascertained and existing facts or circumstances, we might be allowed to predict respecting those which would have taken place; it is more than merely probable, that Spain must have sustained very deep and lasting injury from that war, which was thus unexpectedly and suddenly averted.

The naval power of England, which at no period of past time, had ever been so expeditiously or vigorously called into action: the spirit and unanimity which prevailed throughout the kingdom: the acknowledged energy and capacity of the Administration: the very nature of the war in which we were ready to engage, which must have been not only offensive, but directed to parts of the globe peculiarly calculated to inflame the ardor of the assailants, by prospects of wealth and plunder: the defenceless and unprotected state of many of the Spanish colonies in both hemispheres: the anarchy, and consequent incapacity

of

of France, to extend any prompt and effectual support to the Crown of Spain: even the less important, but distressful and perplexing embarrassments, resulting from the earthquake which demolished the fortress of Oran upon the coast of Africa, almost precisely at the same time when the Emperor of Morocco commenced hostilities against the Catholic King: this combination of causes or events, in which there appears to be no exaggeration, may perhaps, without the imputation of national partiality, justify an opinion, that the Spanish monarchy was snatched by the wise and yielding policy of its Minister, from evils and calamities of no common description.

While, however, I anticipate these advantages, which might probably have resulted from war, under the circumstances already enumerated; it is unquestionable, that to a country so deeply involved in debt, no series of conquests which the wildest imagination can suppose, had they even been realized, could have compensated for the misfortunes inseparably connected with hostilities. Peace, even though only obtained upon the most moderate, and barely equitable terms, must, to every reflecting mind, have been far preferable to the acquisition of all the provinces, which Cortez ever conquered, or Pizarro subdued. But the " Convention" recently signed, while on one hand it made ample reparation and restitution to the injured Crown, and plundered subjects of Great Britain; on the other, opened new and unexplored sources of wealth and commerce. After having been submitted to the inspection and investigation of the people of England, during many weeks: after having received the most authentic attestations of public gratitude and satisfaction, in addresses to the Throne, from the great corporate bodies of London, Edinburgh, and Bristol; necessarily composed of persons highly sensible to, and highly enlightened upon, the commercial interests of the country: after having been finally discussed cuffed with all the feverity of political criticifm, in the two Houfes of Parliament, and attained the fanction of decided approbation in both: having undergone thefe rigorous difquifitions upon its merits, the " Convention " may be examined, like any other fact in the Englifh annals, with the candour, impartiality, and temper of hiftory.

That Great Britain has obtained by it points and objects, hitherto referved or refufed by the Court of Madrid, in every treaty fince the termination of the reign of Philip the Fourth, is inconteftible. Time alone can completely afcertain the value and intrinfic worth of thefe conceffions, which are, in a great degree, dependant on the induftry and enterprize exerted, in converting them to national advantage. That jealous and tenacious power, which originally difcovered and conquered the New World, over which fhe has always endeavoured to draw the deepeft veil, while fhe excluded every European ftate from any participation in her

vaft

vast acquisitions; has, for the first time, receded from her high and exclusive pretensions. The pretended donation of the See of Rome, and all the antiquated claims which long prescription had rendered venerable, have been for ever relinquished and abandoned by the present Convention. The navigation of the Pacific Ocean is, in effect, declared to be as free as that of the Atlantic. The right, claimed by England, of pursuing the fishery on those parts of the coast of South America, unoccupied and uncolonized by Spain, is not only avowed: but a vast tract of the Magellanic regions, on either side of Cape Horn, comprizing the whole coast below the most southern settlement already made by the Spaniards, is declared to be free to both countries, for every purpose of temporary accommodation; while the two Crowns are equally interdicted and restrained, from forming future permanent establishments on that inhospitable shore. In return for this liberal and ample concession, England submits to the equitable

ble demand, of not permitting her vessels to approach within ten leagues of the coasts and countries, actually occupied by Spain upon the Pacific Ocean.

On the North West Coast of America, the original discovery, occupancy, and sovereignty of which, appear to furnish matter of infinite doubt and discussion, still greater advantages are secured by the Convention. Without recapitulating the primary ground of dispute, upon which clear and immediate satisfaction is stipulated: the whole continent, north of the settlements already possessed by Spain, is left open to both nations; with only a reciprocal right of entry for purposes of trade, into the ports or places which either may occupy.

The same general and equal principle is laid down as the basis of accommodation, in the southern and northern hemisphere, and forms the predominant feature of the treaty. It was not denied by the Minister, and it was justly asserted by his opponents, when the Convention was agitated in the House of Commons, that to render

render it perfect, and exempt from future possible misinterpretation, a precise limit should have been drawn, both on the coast of North and South America. But the evils inseparable from a prolongation of the dispute, must have so greatly outweighed the benefit to be derived from any line of demarcation which could have been instantly settled, that no possible censure can be affixed on that account; since its expediency was not more obvious, than its immediate execution was difficult and impracticable. Nor can it be reasonably doubted, that where so clear a principle is by mutual consent established, no essential obstacle can arise, in the course of future negotiations between the two Courts, for the final settlement of their respective boundaries.

To complete this great act of public benefit and national glory, it only remained to meet the expence occasioned by it, with promptitude and alacrity. The Minister, so far from avoiding or protracting that necessary, but painful and arduous task, followed the Convention, with the immediate

diate production of the accounts respecting the naval and military armaments, and the pecuniary impositions which he meant to propose for their speedy liquidation. Not more distinguished by the magnitude and energy of his preparations to humble the monarchy of Spain, when war appeared inevitable; than characterised by the most salutary and severe œconomy, when that necessity no longer existed; his enlarged and active mind overcame the difficulties, by which common statesmen are impeded. He proposed to raise, not merely the interest of the debt recently incurred; but to extinguish the principal itself, in the space of four years, though amounting to above three millions sterling. The effect of so judicious and provident a measure, which must equally evince the magnanimity of the Minister from whom it originated, and the resources of the country which adopted it, will be felt through every kingdom of Europe. It is not exceeded by any of the acts of wisdom, found in the annals of Elizabeth,

beth, when the counsels of England were directed by the foresight and policy of a Burleigh. It is without precedent since the beginning of the present century, and is calculated to excite the admiration and incredulity of future times.

The day, upon which Mr. Pitt submitted to Parliament a system, so calculated for general advantage, was distinguished by another act, which might have rendered illustrious a person, less conspicuously eminent above his fellow citizens. The garter, which was conferred by the Sovereign upon Lord Chatham, evinced the indifference or superiority of the Minister to the highest external decoration and distinction; as powerfully, as his renunciation of a lucrative office in favour of Colonel Barré, at a much earlier period of his administration, had proved his disinterestedness and contempt of emolument.

As it seems hardly possible to have made greater sacrifices, so perhaps, it is difficult to select any example in modern times, of so early an acquisition of that glory

glory, which is the juſt reward of rectitude and talents. Whether the names of Clarendon, of Godolphin, or of Pelham, can be placed in any degree of compariſon or competition with that of Pitt, it may be left to poſterity to determine. But it is competent to the hiſtorian of the preſent age, to aſſert and to prove, that at no period ſince the reſtoration of monarchy in the perſon of Charles the Second, has this country permanently attained to ſo high a point of ſolid greatneſs and importance, as ſhe enjoys at the preſent moment. We ſhould ſearch in vain for any traces of national conſideration or honor, in the profligate annals of that diſſolute and dependent Prince, whom I have juſt named; or in the bigotted and tranſitory reign of his leſs criminal, but more unfortunate ſucceſſor. Shall we diſcover greater ſubject for pride and exultation, even under the temperate and elective government of William the Third?

Whatever obligations we may owe to the Prince of Orange, as our deliverer from civil and spiritual tyranny, his arms were constantly restrained by the Generals, as his measures were uniformly defeated by the policy and power, of Louis the Fourteenth.

After a perpetual and unequal struggle, in which her commerce was almost annihilated, and in which the solitary laurels of the Boyne and of La Hogue, were contrasted with the annual defeats received on the Continent, and in the Channel, Great Britain nearly sunk under the exertion. Though the peace of Ryswick produced a short and delusive calm, yet the Crown of Spain, in violation of the most solemn renunciations, was quietly transferred, in the year 1700, on the extinction of the Spanish branch of the House of Austria, to a Prince of France: while the last hours of William were occupied by ineffectual efforts, to prevent the fatal consequences of an act, incontestably injurious to, or subversive of the security, interests, and greatness of England.

It must be admitted, that the female reign

reign which succeeded, so long as it was conducted by the counsels of Godolphin, and the genius of Marlborough, presents a striking picture of military glory, and successive triumphs. The Court of Versailles, accustomed to confer, condescended to solicit for peace; and Torcy, at Gertruydenburg, in 1709, exhibited the humiliating sight of a Minister of Louis the Fourteenth, prostrate before England and Holland. But the imprudence or presumption of an Administration, intoxicated with prosperity, and unmindful of the changes of human affairs, allowed the moment to elapse, in which the safety and interests of their country might have been for ever secured, on the most durable foundations. The horizon soon became darkened, and the prospect obscured by clouds.

Villars rescued France from her state of danger and distress, while Oxford and Bolingbroke disgraced the government, and accelerated the death of their feeble mistress, by measures of pusillanimity, and breaches of national faith. The

trophies

trophies of Blenheim and of M^aIplaquet were obliterated by the defeat of Denain, and the peace of Utrecht: the Houſe of Auſtria was betrayed in that diſhonourable treaty; and the evening of a reign, ſo diſtinguiſhed and ſo ſplendid, cloſed in weakneſs, and is only recollected with regret.

If the annals of the laſt Princeſs of the Stuart line afford ſo little matter for hiſtoric praiſe, it is not in the labyrinth of Continental Politics and alliances, which characteriſed and compoſed thoſe of George the Firſt, that we can look for topics of eulogium, or ſubjects for admiration. The naval victory, obtained by Byng in 1718, over the Spaniſh fleet in the Faro of Meſſina, however brilliant and deciſive; ſo far from being productive of any advantage to the nation, counteracted every principle of wiſe and judicious policy. It ſtands contraſted with the fatal bankruptcy of the South Sea year; with the melancholy ſacrifice of Hoſier's devoted ſquadron, under the walls of Porto Bello; with a dereliction of the in-

tereſts

terests and honour of the Crown of England, rendered subservient to injurious predilections, and foreign acquisitions.

The commencement of the reign of George the Second, conducted, as the greater part of that of his father had been, by the counsels of Walpole, discloses scarcely a more exhilarating prospect. It was, indeed, pacific: but this peace was the ignominious and supine insecurity of James; not the dignified and martial tranquillity of Elizabeth. I am at a loss to find, in the present century, any portion of time less distinguished by wisdom and vigor; or during which, Great Britain was fallen into more complete insignificance, than in that interval which elapsed from the death of George the First in 1727, to the close, of Sir Robert Walpole's administration, in 1742. Though the subservient fleet of this country escorted the younger son of Philip the Fifth, from Barcelona into Italy: though we facilitated and advanced the grandeur of the House of Bourbon: though we tamely submitted to the acts of violence, exercised by Spain against our commerce in all the American seas: though we abandoned the Emperor Charles the Sixth, to the united force of France, Spain, and Sardinia, who dismembered Naples and Sicily from the dominions of the House of Austria, in so unequal a contest: though, in order that the measure of incapacity and misconduct should be complete, we even permitted Louis the Fifteenth, by incorporating the Dutchy of Lorrain with his hereditary possessions, to cement and perfect the French greatness; yet these mighty and numerous concessions did not conciliate affection, or procure respect. Versed in the arts of Parliamentary address, and the science of domestic venality, but conscious of his incapacity to conduct the vessel through the storm which impended; Walpole, when he had exhausted every endeavour, to detain his Sovereign and his country in disgraceful neutrality, reluctantly resigned the reigns of power, which he had held too long for the honor of his master, or the glory and advantage of England.

Pelham,

Pelham, after a short interval, succeeded. His Administration, though neither fortunate and successful in war, nor secure and undisturbed in peace, yet was rendered respectable, by the lustre of his private and personal virtues. The inglorious campaigns of Fontenoy, and of La Feldt: the defeats of the allied army in Flanders, followed by the capture of Bergen-op-Zoom, and the siege of Maestricht: the peace of Aix la Chapelle, humiliating and injurious to Great Britain: the ravages, or hostilities, continued to be exercised by France against our colonies in America and the East Indies, even subsequent to that treaty: these subjects of general complaint and dissatisfaction, which clouded the Ministry of Pelham, consoled the nation for his loss, when removed by death in 1754, from the superintendance of public affairs.

The short remainder of the reign of George the Second, was equally calamitous and disgraceful, 'till that memorable and brilliant, but transitory æra, preceding its final termination, when the genius of Pitt renewed the glories and successes so long forgotten. The loss of Minorca, and the ignominious convention of Closter-seven, were erased by the successive conquests of Martinico, Canada, Plassey, Beslisle, and the Havanna. But, the demise of the Sovereign, in 1760, and the transfer of ministerial authority which succeeded, prevented the beneficial consequences, naturally to have been expected from this chain of victories. A peace, which never can be sufficiently reprobated, and in which the ignorance of the interests of the nation, was only exceeded by the dereliction of the honor of the Crown, restored to the two branches of the House of Bourbon, those provinces and possessions, of which they had been deprived by the Earl of Chatham.

I shall not enumerate the fleeting phantoms of Administration, which annually appeared and vanished; nor attempt to describe that period which elapsed, from the resignation of Lord Bute, to the year 1770, when the reins of power were delegated to Lord North. There are certainly few events, included within that portion of time, which can induce us to lament that it was not of longer duration. With still greater reason, I wish to draw a veil across the series of errors, incapacity, and misconduct, which preceded and produced that fatal war, terminated by the emancipation of America; and which still blazed in every quarter of the globe, at the æra when these memoirs commence.

From the elevation on which we are placed, it affords a sort of melancholy pleasure, to look down upon the anarchy and calamity, which endear the present Government, by a comparison with that state from which we have escaped. The actual situation of this country realizes the warmest wish of a Minister, or a Sovereign, to whom the prosperity and glory of England are supremely dear. That object which William vainly sought to attain; which Godolphin and Marlborough allowed to escape; and which the Earl of Chatham was not permitted to accomplish; has been

been referved for the prefent age to behold. The monarchies of France and Spain have been fucceffively humbled and reftrained, without the neceffity of having recourfe to the fword. Great Britain, at the conclufion of 1790, is become by general confent, the acknowledged Arbitrefs of Europe; and to her poffeffion of external confideration and refpect, unites every internal fource of wealth and felicity.

From the furvey of fo auguft and animating a fcene, it is natural to turn our eyes towards the picture exhibited by France, at the prefent moment. The convulfions which have agitated that diftracted country fince the month of October 1789, though fometimes apparently fufpended or extinguifhed, yet may poffibly revive with augmented violence. The laft fourteen months feem to have been alternately diftinguifhed, by acts of feftivity and of flaughter; by the pageant of a Fœderation, in the "Champ de Mars" at Paris, where the national freedom was folemnly recognized by a captive and degraded Sovereign;

reign; and by the memorable carnage of Nancy, which so quickly followed. It is perhaps impossible for the wisest statesman to predict the eventual consequence of these conflicting causes; or to hazard a decided opinion on the final result, as yet concealed in futurity, and obscured by so many contradictory appearances. The depression and humiliation of the clergy; the sale of the ecclesiastical property; the annihilation of the orders of nobility, which were almost coeval with the times of Clovis and of Pharamond; the abolition of the peerage; the renewal of the dangerous experiments of Law, and the creation of a paper currency, nearly as destitute of solid support, as was the system of that celebrated minister: These extraordinary operations, or measures of government, in a great degree without precedent in the history of modern European nations, have not yet sufficiently unfolded and developed their full effect, to enable the philosopher and the historian to confer on them his censure, or his admiration.

It

It has not even hitherto been afcertained or exemplified, fince the extinction of the Roman freedom by Marius and Sylla, that a people whofe numbers exceed twenty millions, are capable of being permanently governed under a free conftitution. Nor has mankind yet feen any inftance of a capital, and a country, habituated for ages to defpotifm, funk in pleafures, loft to public principle, deftitute even of the forms of external refpect for the national religion, and only intoxicated with the fpeculations of a diftempered and vifionary philofophy, which ever afpired or attained to a well-regulated and wifely-cemented Liberty.

It was not in fuch a ftate of morals or of fociety, that the Athenians broke the fetters of arbitrary power, when roufed by Harmodius and Ariftogiton. The elder Brutus bore no fimilarity either to Mirabeau, or to La Fayette. Rome vainly affaffinated her Dictator, when public virtue was no longer to be found in the fenate, or among the people. The Mountaineers of Switzerland, who threw off the

the yoke of the House of Austria; and the oppressed peasants of the Low Countries, who revolted from the tyranny of Philip the Second, were poor, hardy, and martial. The English Parliament, which opposed, and ultimately vanquished Charles the First, called upon a nation, which however inflamed by fanaticism, was unsubdued by luxury, and uncorrupted by venality. Times of effeminacy and refinement have not hitherto been found to produce a plant, of so hardy and vigorous a nature, as Freedom; and if we are destined to see in the history of France, an example of this extraordinary contradiction to the result of all experience, it will be a striking lesson of the insufficiency and fallibility, of human wisdom or observation.

The time which has elapsed since the Revolution of July, 1789, has not been sufficient, to ascertain all its consequences, or to ripen and mature the many causes, which may still shake the freedom of France, before it attains to solidity. The yielding and

and paffive conduct of the King, which has fo powerfully operated to produce fubmiffion in the two orders of the nobility and clergy, may be overborne by events, or may be affected by the advice and counfels of thofe who approach his perfon. The natural levity, and characteriftic inconftancy of the nation, may conduce to make them weary of a poffeffion, which however ineftimable in its nature, is neither to be attained, nor preferved, without unremitting vigilance and exertion. The ceffation or ruin of many branches of trade, neceffarily refulting from the late convulfions: the feverity of the taxes, which a free Government is compelled to exact, in common with the moft defpotic Monarch: the long habits of unconditional fubmiffion, fo forcible in their operation upon the mind and character: All thefe principles may ferment, and ultimately burft into action.

To the internal fources of change and commotion, external ones may unite. Of the feven fugitive Princes of the Blood, who pre- cipitately

cipitately abandoned their country at the commencement of the national troubles, only one, the Prince of Conti, has yet ventured to revisit Paris, or submitted to take the Civic Oath, imposed by the new constitution. The malcontents, assembled at Turin round the person of the Count d'Artois, aided by the capacity and resources of Calonne, and ready to be led on by Maillebois, menace the duration of the National Assembly. Even though these storms were dissipated, yet the Courts of Vienna and Madrid cannot be supposed to look with pleasure, or approbation, on the fallen condition of Louis the Sixteenth; and would, probably, aid with more than wishes, any effectual struggles which might be made for the restoration of his antient prerogatives. These reflections and considerations may inspire some reasonable doubt, respecting the final issue of the subversion of the Royal Power, and the permanency of a free constitution in France.

Whatever may be the result, and though liberty should even ultimately triumph, its attainment has been accompanied with, at least, a temporary diminution, approaching to total fufpenfion, of the political ftrength, importance, and confideration of the kingdom, as a European ftate. The energy and activity of the Crown have been withdrawn; and a fpirit of licentioufnefs, the moft fatal to every national and public effort, has prevailed throughout all the naval and military departments. The French colonies in the Weft Indies are engaged in civil war, or become a prey to infurrection and anarchy. The frontiers, towards Germany, Savoy, and Spain, are either expofed to infult and invafion; or protected by troops, upon whofe fteady attachment and fidelity, after the late defection from their Prince, no fecure reliance can be placed. That powerful monarchy, which for near a century and a half has infpired terror, and whofe reftlefs ambition has been fo dangerous to every furrounding country: which has twice, during that time, nearly fubjected Holland; which placed Philip the Fifth on the Spanifh throne in 1700,

and

and raised an Elector of Bavaria to the Imperial dignity, at a still more recent period: that power, occupied in endless metaphysical disquisitions upon the rights of men, or employed in desperate projects of revenue and finance, appears not only to be incapable of invading the repose of her neighbours, but even of providing for her own internal safety and tranquillity.

Such is the striking contrast, which the two monarchies of France and England actually present. The one, struggling through difficulties, to complete a system of liberty; and attempting to renovate her disordered finances, plunged into almost irremediable confusion. The other, enjoying all the advantages of established order; conducted by a Government equally vigorous and popular; meeting every pecuniary embarrassment or imposition, with new and unexampled resources; strengthening her credit; and extending her commerce, while she covers the ocean with her navy, and spreads the glory of her name over every quarter of the earth.

I am arrived at that period, where the present work must necessarily terminate. I am conscious that it is only an outline; but the events of which I have treated, are not sufficiently removed, to admit of minute enquiry, or profound investigation. Yet, this imperfect production may perhaps serve to light the steps of some future Hume or Gibbon, to whom genius shall delegate the sublime task, of recording and perpetuating the English annals. My object has been only to commemorate the facts and characters, which have made the deepest impression on my memory and understanding, while a spectator of their full effect; and to stamp them with the genuine sentiment which they excited, of approbation or censure. "Statui res gestas "Populi Romani," says Sallust, "carp- "tim, ut quæque memoria digna vide- "bantur, perscribere; eo magis, quod "mihi a Spe, Metu, partibus Reipublicæ, "animus liber erat."

Whether I may be esteemed altogether exempt from the emotions, disclaimed by
the

the Roman writer, I muft leave to thofe who fhall perufe this work, to determine. It is difficult to diveft ourfelves of the predilections, which almoft neceffarily arife in our minds, when engaged in the recital or defcription of fcenes, acted in ages and countries the moft remote. It would rather imply a degree of apathy, and defect of feeling, than any fuperiority to common and vulgar prejudice, if I could furvey with the fame tranquillity, the calamities, which only a few years fince, threatened the deftruction of England, and the prefent elevated ftate of fecurity which we enjoy: or if in relating them, I fhould allow no portion of enthufiafm to mix with the veneration, always due to hiftoric truth. Gratitude is naturally excited in every generous breaft, by private benefits: but the Sovereign, or the Minifter, who are the benefactors of nations, kindle, even in the hiftorian who tranfmits to future times the events of their government, a venial partiality; nor can the

reign

reign of Trajan and Aurelius be written with the fame indifference, as we feel in defcribing the gluttony of Vitellius, or the crimes of Caracalla.

F I N I S.

ANOTHER SKETCH

OF THE

REIGN OF GEORGE III.

FROM THE YEAR 1780 TO 1790.

BEING

AN ANSWER TO

A SKETCH, &c.

PART THE FIRST.

LONDON:
Printed for James Ridgway, York-Street.
1791.

*T*HE *Author laments that the crowd of important matter which occupies the beginning of the period which this Sketch proposes to describe, as well as the lateness of the season for publication, does not permit him to deduce his history beyond the dissolution of the parliament in* 1784; *the work will be comprized in two parts: and the Second Part, which will be the most important from the quantity as well as the quality of the subjects which it will treat of, will be published towards the close of the year, and will be extended to whatever is comprised in the present session of parliament.*

ANOTHER SKETCH
OF THE
REIGN OF GEORGE III.

TO narrate events in order to afford materials "to some future Hume or Gibbon, to whom Genius shall delegate the sublime task of recording and perpetuating the English annals," is certainly an undertaking both modest in its purpose, and useful in its execution: and though posterity may not be able to acknowledge this obligation, on account of the uncertainty or the oblivion of its author, yet a present retribution will not fail to attend such an endeavour; and contemporary gratitude will bestow the praise, which the judgment of futurity will not indeed have the means of securing.

But if its laudable to clear the way of the historian, whose steps are doubtfully, though cautiously traced through the intricacies of conjecture, or quite obstructed by the darkness of ignorance,—surely he deserves to be extolled by rapturous gratitude who shall recal the unwary traveller from the paths of error, who shall retard or stop his hardy progress by persuasion, by intreaty, by authority—who shall call aloud " quit the road, unhappy that you are! which you now pursue—it is not among the flowers of panegyric, it is not among the illusions that fancy creates and only interest adopts, that you will find that truth which you seek. Check your rein; proceed not —examine, doubt, consult, judge; weigh motives, trace causes, consider actions relatively to characters, to conjunctures, to nature: and though the evidence of tradition should perplex or fail you, philosophy shall yet shed a friendly light, and conduct your steps."

It is hardly necessary to state, that the avowed intention of this little essay or treatise is to obviate some misrepresentation of things and of characters which have gone abroad in a book or pamphlet, intitled, " A Sketch of the

Reign of George the Third," to refer effects to their proper causes, and to substitute truth for panegyric.

The author proposes, moreover, in the course of his undertaking, to make some observations concerning the nature and the end of government in general, and the nature of the British Government in particular. What is its theory! what its practice! what its capacity for duration! what is its essential character! and what the influence of this character in the production of a system of conduct, which, when it has continued uniform for a length of time, must be the effect of a constant cause. This latter object, however, he shall refer to the second part of this treatise, and he hopes to receive the indulgence of the public, if he does not make a hasty production of opinions that require much reflection in their adoption, and much delicacy in their promulgation.

In tracing the affairs of men it will generally be found, that any great deviation from the rules of prudence and of justice may be considered as a kind of first link in that continued chain of events which is certain to terminate in some fatal catastrophe, and though properly

properly speaking there is no such thing in all human affairs as a first cause, that which is called so, being as strictly dependant upon some event which has preceded it, as its own immediate effect is dependant upon it, and that which is called the final effect or catastrophe being most certainly a necessary cause with respect to some succeeding event; yet, because, the connection in either case is not quite so apparent to the dull sense of man, as it is with respect to all the intermediate events; so we term this continued sensible chain a series, and from hence the epoch of the historian receives its denomination. That the American war was a measure of impolicy the event has sufficiently demonstrated, that it was a measure founded in injustice, and in a spirit of domination, is yet a question among those whom national partiality would incline to a favourable judgment, though it is no question among those whom the same motive would incline to a contrary decision: but leaving this discussion aside, certain it is that the surrender of the southern enemy at York-Town was a kind of final effect of that measure, since from that time a new order of things has arisen, by which

a difa different object is proposed, and of which the events that now pass before us form a part of another connected chain or series.

What were the motives which induced Lord North to resign his situation of minister in March 1782, and subsequent to that surrender, it is not perhaps so difficult a task to conjecture as the sagacious author of the Sketch seems to imagine. That minister probably considered that the war in which the nation had been unhappily involved with America was the prevailing feature, and indeed the grand principle of his administration, of which all the other parts were but subordinate, and dependant as it were upon that measure: when therefore the House of Commons manifested its disapprobation of that war, when a resolution was carried against its continuance, and when it was even not opposed when moved, that which ever of his majesties ministers should advise its continuance, should be deemed enemies of the country, and of his majesty, when all this was done not in a single movement of passion, not upon the sudden impulse of a great and grievous calamity, but after much intervention of time, much temperate

rate deliberation, and by many succeffive resolutions, we can find but little to wonder at or admire, wherefore a minister whose whole administration had been thus involved in one general censure, from whom the confidence of Parliament had been withdrawn, and who consequently would have been able to do no one ministerial act, should resign his office, should retire into the ranks, nor think it painful to submit to a necessity which he could not control.

It therefore required no very great portion of sagacity even for the author of the Sketch to discover the motives of the resignation of Lord North, when he found that his measures had been disapproved of by the Commons, and that he was deemed the author, the instigator, or the instrument, by which the nation had fallen into so great a calamity. Nor though the favour and SUPPORT OF THE CROWN had remained to him, should " the announcing his resignation or stripping himself of the insignia of office," under these circumstances of public disapprobation " have so much astonished the audience as to make them doubt the fact of which they were witnesses,"

But

But yet that minister did not wait for any extreme resolutions before he relinquished his place, *he* did not set the gratification of his ambition or his lust of power against the sense directly expressed of the representatives of the nation, *he* did not stake his continuance in office against the order and the tranquillity of the country upon the credit of the moderation of a popular assembly;—but with the dignity of a man, and with the virtue of a patriot, he resigned his office, rather than he would countenance so pernicious a precedent that it could be *retained*, although it might be granted, without the concurrence of the people expressed by its only organ, namely, the House of Commons legally and constitutionally assembled and existing.

It has been frequently asserted, and it has been too often proved by experience, that the conduct of political men is more directed by interest or convenience, more guided by conjunctures, than governed by any general immutable principles of public virtue; and such deviations from moral rectitude so long as the public only is concerned, are *imputed* with levity and received with indulgence, though if if they should affect the private transactions of life, contempt or reproach would be a never-failing consequence of the base proceeding. If we seek for the cause of a distinction where none ought to exist, or where it ought to exist in an inverse manner; for the practice of private morality must be at last traced up to public utility as its proper and original source, and public utility is indeed directly and immediately affected by the practice of public virtue; I say, if we seek for the causes of this distinction, we shall discover them in the vanity, and in the pride and in the desire of superiority which are implanted in mankind. No particular injury can be done to an individual without vesting in that individual a right of complaint and reproach, a right of which nature will compel the exercise, and the exercise of which is not very well calculated to gratify the vanity, and feed the pride of him who is the object of it. But in the case of a public injury no particular individual has a right to complain beyond the rest of his fellow citizens, and as the universality of an injury prevents an insult, so one great, the greatest source of human resentment, is not concerned in the revenge.

Hence

Hence it is that private promises are ever deemed sacred even by those who make no scruple of violating public faith, not indeed from the virtue of their characters, but from the vice of their nature; hence too those political men who, while they have been in opposition to a powerful administration, have maintained with great zealousness the expediency of a retrenchment in the public expenditure, of a reduction of places, and of a diminution of influence; when they have been seated on the side of power, have forgot their airy promises, have retrenched no part of the public expenditure, have reduced no places, and have diminished no influence, governed by the same interest, that under different circumstances and in a different conjuncture had betrayed them into professions which were the effect of a shifting convenience.

The whole nation anxiously wishes for a parliamentary reform: The representation is defective, it is incomplete, and single individuals, by that change to which all human affairs are subject, have possessed themselves gradually, and without effort, of the dearest rights of large bodies of men. What more popular than for a member of sufficient abilities, to come forward to vindicate the injured conſtitution, and to aſſert the claims of the public. But what more for his intereſt too? if he ſucceeds he brings down the miniſter from his vantage ground, and in the ſcramble, I ſhould rather call it the allotment which will now take place, he will have a fair chance in the gratification of an honeſt ambition, in proportion to his talents, and let me add to his virtue too; and his particular merits upon ſuch an occaſion would moſt certainly not be forgotten. But let a fortunate train of circumſtances make this man miniſter: Will he purſue that object of his heart which but now he burned for with all the flames of a lover? Has he not the very means of attaining it? or does the certainty of poſſeſſion impoſe its icy hand upon this ſpecies of deſire, and render him indifferent becauſe it is in his power to be happy. But it is not neceſſary to ſearch for remote cauſes upon ſuch an occaſion. The times have changed, and our opinions alſo have changed. There are diſturbances abroad—there may be diſaffection at home—let us not ſtir up bad humours by the introduction of new things, and

and let us prefer the security of prescription to the dangers of innovation.

In opposition to the foregoing observations concerning political frailty, and the truth of which must be generally acknowledged; let me direct the attention of the reader to the conduct of the administration which immediately succeeded upon the resignation of Lord North. An administration most honourably distinguished by the name of Rockingham; and whose existence though it continued for no more than three months, a circumstance of great exultation to the author of the Sketch, could not be called short, for if duration is relative to succession, that life which is crouded with good acts is both glorious and long.

In order that we may obtaain the clue by which the conduct of this administration was guided, by which its consistency is proved, and its virtue exemplified, it will be necessary to recur to a very memorable event in the former parliament. Upon a question moved by Mr. Dunning, it was carried that the influence of the crown had increased, was increasing, and ought to be diminished. This solemn declaration however of the representatives of the people was attended with no beneficial effects, for a speedy dissolution that his majesty was advised to make, intercepted the advantage which the public would probably have derived from the virtue or the repentance of that parliament: I say the repentance, because it is remarkable that this abstract proposition (and let it be observed once for all, that the term * abstract signifies the result which is obtained

---

* It is to be observed, that the terms abstract, philosophy, metaphysics, &c. have been much confounded of late, and endeavoured to be brought into disrepute by those who could only expect to succeed in perverting reason, by confounding terms. The author of the letter upon the French Revolution, speaking of rights, &c. says, their abstract perfection is their practical defect: now, abstract perfection can only arise from practical excellency; and it is, indeed, from the contemplation and knowledge of individuals alone, that we are able to combine various qualities, so as to complete and harmonize any system whatever, whether of mechanics or of ethics, and the effects and the value of a system so framed, may be most precisely ascertained, by resolving it into its elementary parts. Now it is this capacity, which is in individuals, or in the qualities of individuals, to be combined and adapted, that gives rise to the philosophical expression of fitness of things, an expression which, though Fielding has very successfully ridiculed,

obtained from the contemplation of particulars) was voted by a Parliament that in *no particular* had opposed the measures of the minister; and therefore its theory upon this occasion might be said to be at variance with its practice: a circumstance that adds a very peculiar authority to the proposition which was affirmed; in as much as it is not usual with men to grant any inference from their conduct, which inference implies a censure, unless they are compelled to it by the obligation of truth.

But when his Majesty, *in compliance with the wishes of his people,* had framed a new administration, that was informed by the experience, and guided by the gentle ascendant of the Marquis of Rockingham, and of which, if we consider some at least (unhappily not all) of the other component parts, we shall find genius adorned with simplicity, virtue, tried by perseverance and fortitude, proof

---

ridiculed, by a ludicrous incident in the life of Square, which all my readers will probably recollect, is not the less just upon that account, and this circumstance may serve to prove that ridicule is not always the test of truth.

against

against temptation, and the allurements of interest; the nation was not deceived in the just expectation which it entertained of such men, and we shall see, in this part of our history, a very splendid exception to the inconsistence and perfidy of political men, who make their own convenience the measure of their professions and of their practice.

The disposal of many offices, an extensive patronage, the influence of the treasury, in the election of members of parliament, an influence, the very suspicion of which should be carefully avoided, and its practice abhorred; all these things, as they are advantages on the side of the minister, as they secure friendship by the impulse of gratitude, as they procure support by the allurements of expectation, and as they render parliament dependant by the operation of both, so that administration which should, relinquish whatever, of patronage, is inconsistent with the integrity of the constitution, which should submit the power of doing ill to be retrenched by salutary provisions, while it retained the power of doing good not only by the natural prevalency of good over ill, but by preserving as many supports as would

would crush faction, and render the conduct of affairs easy and enviable, would deserve the thanks of the present age, and would receive the admiration of posterity.

The reader will easily conceive that I allude to two memorable acts that past during that administration, by one of which though it was posterior to the other in date, officers of the revenue were disabled from voting for members of Parliament, and consequently one great fountain of undue influence entirely dried up, to the great benefit of the public, but to the greater ease of that class of citizens who consented to their disqualification when they retained their places, and who are now no longer obliged to sacrifice their prepossessions, their feelings, their friendships, and their conscience at the shrine of power, in order that they might not lose those wages which the discharge of their duty deserved, but only their corruption could secure.

The other act was more particularly known by the name of Mr. Burke's Reform Bill, before it became a law. By this act a saving was made of 72,000l. a year, by the retrenchment of offices; a saving of great importance,

con-

considered in that single view: but of the greatest importance, when considered relatively to its effects in restoring in some degree that independency of parliament, without which the nation, though it may enjoy the form of a free constitution, will, upon that account, be only plunged in a more hopeless slavery.

But, says the author of the Sketch, whose gentle tones have, upon this occasion, sharpened into invective, " This was a Bill which disarmed every succeeding Minister, by leaving him scarcely any objects by which to stimulate activity, or to reward merit and *adherence*. A Bill which, by compelling every Administration, from want of offices, to multiply the peerage, as the only thing left in their power to bestow, and which, if not redressed and repealed, may eventually destroy the balance of the constitution; a Bill, &c. &c."

That the progressive multiplication of the peerage does not only bid fair, but is certain to destroy the balance of the constitution is a point I shall not dispute with the author of the Sketch; and as it is one of the very few points, I might say the only one, in which I do do agree with that author, I am the more particular in stating this conformity of opinion, as well for its singularity, as because it is some proof that I do not disagree with him necessarily, but only because I think I have reason to do so upon all other occasions. But though I admit of his conclusion, respecting the danger of the constitution, from a multiplication of the peerage; yet the other conclusion, for the sake of which the former was inadvertently made, namely, that therefore Mr. Burke's Reform Bill merited the detestation of any other description of persons, but of those who have lost every honest feeling, in a base subserviency to a Court or to a Minister, I do most strenuously oppose.

When that Bill was proposed, it did not occur to those (nor, thank God, has the case yet occured) who supported and carried it through, that at any distance of time, a hardy Minister would arise, who, careless of every consideration of public good, should maintain his private interests by advising an intemperate exercise of a prerogative which must be attended with such fatal effects; who should secure his situation of

Minister, by endangering the liberties of the people, and should save what was personal to himself, by wasting, with a shameless prodigality, the constitution of his country. Certainly such apprehensions, so injurious, so little probable in the event, could not be entertained by persons whose hearts were pure, whose intentions were righteous, and whose resources were not of that kind; nor if they had been entertained would they have changed their measures, or have desisted from them: for virtue is still immutable, nor do the good refuse to act because they are afraid of the crimes of the wicked.

But if we are desirous of beholding a truly sublime and affecting spectacle, let us pause for a moment, while we contemplate the conduct of his Majesty at this happy period of his reign, and upon this very occasion. Superior to every pitiful suggestion of a false and selfish policy, erecting no separate interest from that of his people; but feeling that their cause and his own were indissolubly connected, that the ease and prosperity of the one were the proper and only sources of the splendour and happiness of the other, he did not wait for

for an application from his Parliament, he did not confent to the meafure—he demanded it. He faw, without being fhewn, that a reform in fuch a crifis, and in fuch circumftances, was not only proper, but neceffary; and he was a volunteer in the fervice. Nor is his magnanimity without reward: For by how much affection, and love, and gratitude, are more to be coveted than every other poffeffion, by fo much has he gained, inftead of lofing, by the pretended facrifice.

It is doubtlefs in the contemplation of a fcene like this, that our affections, always warm, are moft powerfully excited towards the King*; nor, if we wifh to retain impreffions of the goodnefs of his Majefty's government, fhould we view him at the time when the whole nation was bent upon the termination of the American war, for fuch is the light in which this libeller falfely, and injurioufly reprefents him; as bent upon the profecution of that war, as regardlefs of the

* Page 20, Sketch, &c. " Bent on the profecution of a war, which was founded in the juft rights of his throne, no fymptom of charge or alarm appeared in the Sovereign, &c."

wishes of his people, as erecting an interest separate from theirs, and anxious to sacrifice both to the lust of personal dominion, or of fell revenge.

In this train of affairs, when the nation had a right to look forward with exultation and hope to that change, that a virtuous conduct never fails to operate, certainly, but gradually, upon the stubbornness and malignity of fortune; the decease of the Marquis of Rockingham, which happened on the 1st of July, 1782, at once closed the scene; and a schism took place in the cabinet, by which the nation was deprived of the services of Mr. Fox, and Lord John Cavendish. It appears that the causes of this disagreement had existed even in the life time of the Marquis, though his authority, and a tenderness for his declining health, had served a little to compose that difference, that was, however, certain to break out soon into an open rupture.

That the majority of the cabinet had shewn some disposition to depart from that simplicity of conduct, by the expectation of which they had been first recommended to office, and that views of domination and conquest, quite inconsistent confiftent with the refolutions that had been the bafis of the public exiftence of thofe ungrateful men, had began to mingle in their councils, there can, I think, be little doubt, as well from the ftatement of Mr. Fox when he declared the reafons of his refignation, (though perhaps he did not exprefsly fay this) as from certain ambiguous expreffions, fuch as that, " when the independance of America was granted, the fun of Britain was fet for ever," and the like, which fell about that time from the Earl of Shelburne, who had fecured to himfelf, with great addrefs and management, the office of firft Lord of the Treafury; and being then the refponfible Minifter, it was not to be fuppofed, that, entertaining fuch fentiments, he would proceed in a fyftem, by which fuch a mighty ruin was to be effected.

There is then every reafon, as far as probability will determine conjecture, to believe that the old fyftem was to be revived, and that the nation was to be again plunged in all thofe horrors from whence it had fo lately feemed to have efcaped; but the refignation of Mr. Fox, and of Lord John Cavendifh,

together

together with the defection of some who adhered personally to those two Gentlemen, and of more, who were guided as well by reason as by authority, and the alarm of all considerate men, declared in the most unequivocal manner the danger and the impracticability of proceeding in such measures, if any such had been adopted by the cabinet, or plotted by some of its leading and prevailing members, which latter there is the greatest reason, from circumstances, to suppose was the fact.

The resignation of Lord John Cavendish made room for Mr. Pitt to succeed to the situation of Chancellor of the Exchequer, a gentleman, who from his appointment at such an early age, for he was then scarcely twenty-five years old, to so high an office, and whose subsequent appointment with a small interval, to the highest, which he now continues to fill, have rendered him the object of that kind of admiration that is the sudden and never failing effect of any singular appearance.

In all governments, in which the people have any share in the conduct of affairs, the talent of public speaking, as it confers the greatest possible superiority in popular assemblies,

blies, upon him who poffeffes it moft eminently, is fure to be cultivated with the greateft care and induftry: it is however maintained by Cicero, whofe opinion upon this fubject will be deemed of the laft importance, that notwithftanding the pains and induftry of many, combined with the genius of fome, the efforts of all have fallen fhort, and that there is no fuch thing in nature as a perfect orator; and he concludes upon the whole that there never will be fuch a phenomenon. Now fuch a conclufion with refpect to Cicero himfelf is undoubtedly a juft one; but how far other men may be warranted in adopting it, is a matter which I think deferves fome little examination.

For, as the minds of men are varioufly modified, as fome are of a greater capacity than others, fo is there a different ftandard of judgment in each. All judgment is by comparifon, nor can we appreciate excellence of any kind, but by referring it, and comparing it, to fomething known. But the intellectual powers of any man, or what is the effect of the intellectual powers of any man, fuch as eloquence, for the greateft part, is, can only be referred,

referred, by the perfon who judges of it, to his own capacity, (I do not fpeak of attainment, for capacity exceeds attainment*, it cannot be referred to any thing external, for that which is external being not known, cannot be a ftandard of judgment. Hence it was that Cicero whofe genius was the greateft, and the continual application and exercife of whofe mental powers, had carried his attainments beyond thofe not only of his cotemporaries, but of thofe who had ever preceded him in

---

* When I fay that capacity exceeds attainment I muft be underftood to fpeak of that period of the human life, when nature has not yet begun to yield to the illapfes of age, an effect that takes place much later in the mind, than in the body, probably becaufe we have not fo many, nor fuch direct means of corrupting it by intemperance.

And it feems moreover reafonable to think that the quality of the mind which is called tafte, may be refered to capacity. We are often fenfible of, and tafte beauties, in works of genius, which yet we are not able to imitate, but why are we not able to imitate? for it is plain that there muft be at leaft a conformity in the conftitution of the mind that adopts, and the mind that creates an effect. The reafon in this cafe is, becaufe practice is wanting to fecure attainment; the power which nature has given being only a paffive power: which is the precife definition of tafte.

cultivat-

cultivating eloquence; when he fought for an example of a perfect orator, he was obliged to deny its exiftence: doubtlefs he could not pronounce it perfect in others, which he was, himfelf able to excel; nor could he pronounce it perfect in himfelf, from a confcioufnefs that he had not reached the limits of nature, and that there was yet fome interval between his attainments, and his power to attain: a confcioufnefs, with which all but the moft incorrigible blockheads are poffeffed, though none feel it fo fenfibly as thofe who are inbued with that portion of the divine fpirit which is denominated genius. He was therefore obliged, for want of any ground to repofe upon, to take flight into the airy regious of poffibility; and to deny the *actual* exiftence of that, which, from the circumftance of his own excellence, and of his own defect, he could only conceive *poffibly* to exift.

It follows from this, that a perfon of inferior genius, and more limited attainments than the Roman, would be fatisfied of the exiftence of that which the other denied: the fame caufe producing from the different circumftances of each, a different conclufion: he

would

would not send his thoughts out in quest of possibilities; he would receive examples; and these examples would multiply in proportion to the little capacity and few attainments of those who made this matter the subject of their contemplation.

Now oratory in general may be divided into two parts: 1st, into the power that the mind has of calling up and arranging appropriate ideas; 2dly, into the power of expressing those ideas, or into elocution, which latter is the effect principally of habit and of practice, and affords the praise of *industry*; while the former challenges the admiration of *nature*. But oratory being conversant with associations of ideas and their expression, let the ideas be never so vulgar and ordinary, if the elocution is splendid (as those who are poor endeavour to go richly habited) still it is plain that a species of oratory will have been constituted; and I think it may be inferred from what has been said concerning the different standards of judgment, that this species of oratory, however contemptible it may be to some, may yet be extolled by others when they feel that their own

own capacity has been exceeded by the powers of the Rhetor.

Another obfervation that I would wifh to make upon this fubject, and which I truft will not be deemed a contradiction to my former reafonings, is, that elocution, or phrafeology, or the manner of fpeaking, as diftinguifhed from true eloquence, is lefs fitted to meet with approbation among the rude vulgar, than among thofe who have the advantage of fuch an education as gentlemen of the prefent time commonly receive; but who do not poffefs that fimplicity of tafte which is generally the gift of a bountiful nature, though it is fometimes the reward of painful diligence. Thefe who know juft fo much as to be acquainted with the difficulty of public fpeaking, are ftruck with art, the vulgar are pleafed with nature: the tafte of thefe is corrupted or fhackled by a little knowledge; the tafte of the vulgar riots in the freedom of ignorance. Great is the power of eloquence; great the power of the external fenfible marks of eloquence. The pomp of language, the force of emphafis, the length of period, fentences involved in fentences, meaning artfully refembled or plainly expofed, and now a variety

riety and now a repetition of terms—what person whose lips have tasted, but who has not drank deeply of the well of science, but is hurried away by the impetuous movement, and embraces with rapture the gaudy phantom.

I hope I shall be excused if I have engaged in this digression respecting eloquence, and the means by which we form judgments concerning it, and the cause of the difference of those judgments in different men: whatever relates to the art of speaking cannot be unseasonable, when the merits of Mr. Pitt are the subject of discussion. Yet it must be acknowledged, that in stating a case or narration, that Gentleman is easily the first; if indeed he is too minute; yet is not his audience intuitive; nor are his other means less accommodated to his end; if it is not prudent to expose a measure, who so capable of mysterious invelopement; if he does not answer, he decomposes, the arguments of his adversary, strips them of their fatal circumstances, confutes the remainders, and conquers in detail when it is not practicable to engage in the gross. If to these we add a graveness of tone, a pomp of language,

a man-a manner that imposes, an authority that commands; we shall find combined in this minister whatever an anxious nation can desire, to create and to secure its prosperity, and to adorn its annals.

But let not the voice of prejudice with a treacherous malignity conceal or obscure the merit whose existence it regrets, while it expatiates with the fondest pleasure upon the faults or defects of a hated object. Far, far from me be such a cause, or such an effect. I have even heard with delight, when Mr. Fox, having exhausted his subject with every variety of reasoning, that a capacious and a well stored mind could furnish; when having clearly satisfied all, *he* alone has appeared not to be satisfied; and stretching beyond the limits of possible conviction, has fallen short of his natural effort, and has not rejected arguments that were not necessary or that were weak—I say, I have heard with delight upon such an occasion the skilful ingenuity, and have applauded the dexterous discernment, of the Chancellor of the Exchequer; who has left no part of the adverse argument unexplored, has avoided or just *seemed* to answer what was

strong;

ſtrong ; but has ſeized upon what was weak, as his proper prey; has attacked, has ſubdued, has expoſed in triumph, has afflicted with a painful and lingering death, the object of his mercileſs victory, and has obtained a praiſe, not ſcanty, from the exuberance of his antagoniſt.

But to return : an adminiſtration which originated in fraud, which ſubſiſted in weakneſs, and which proceeded in folly, could not be long-lived. While the Marquis of Rockingham was yet living and miniſter, one of the moſt ſignal naval victories that the hiſtory of this country can boaſt was obtained in the Weſt-Indies, under the auſpices of Admiral Rodney; and what ſeemed to render it more important, was the circumſtance of its being gained in parts, where only diſgrace had hitherto attended the Britiſh arms, and the aſcendancy of France had been completely eſtabliſhed by her continued and ſucceſſive conqueſts.

St. Chriſtopher, the glory and the reproach of the Britiſh commander whom Rodney joined, had but a little before ſurrendered to the fortune and perſeverance of the Marquis de Boullé

Boullé after a siege of considerable duration. When that island was first attacked, the English admiral quitting his station to windward came to its relief, though St. Christopher is situated low down in that chain of islands whose direction, in general, from South to North, bends with no slight deviation to the westward before you approach that scene of fruitless gallantry. With a fleet much inferior, but by a series of masterly manœuvres, he obtained possession of the very ground, where the French fleet had anchored, but which had slipped upon his approach, in order to seize the easy prey. But this ground was at the extremest distance from the fortress that was attacked, and where there was no communication, how should there be any relief? Had the British commander instead of remaining until the fortress surrendered, in the very spot where the prudence of Mr. de Grasse, would by a peculiar inconsistency of sentiment, have allotted him his station, returned from whence he came, as soon as he found his object could not accomplished; the expectation of Vandreuil, and the fear of Rodney, (and the arrival of both was awaited at that very juncture,)

juncture,) would not have suffered the French commander to waste a precious time by continuing to leeward, when the junction of the one or the capture of the other, or both, would be the necessary consequence of the return of the British fleet to a windward and customary cruize or station : and the conquest of St. Christopher must have been abandoned by the French long before the time that was necessary to complete it, to secure an advantage which was essential, and to avoid a danger which would have been fatal.

But by the victory of Lord Rodney a mighty change was wrought in the affairs of those parts: those who had before attacked were not now able to defend, and that force which had diffused itself in conquest, though it had been concentered in a single effort, would have ill resisted a vigourous assailant.

It is here necessary that I should a little dilate upon the nature of the victory of Lord Rodney, and that I should state what might have been its advantages in order to ascertain in this period of our history, how far fortune was seconded by conduct, and to determine in this particular the merits of an administration

tion in which the sublime and early talents of a youthful Chancellor of the Exchequer were conjoined with the experience of a practised statesman: for it is to be remembered that this administration was publicly established in a very little time after the *intelligence* of that victory arrived, though its power of framing any system of action was probably established before it could have arrived its predominancy, being the very cause of the resignation of Mr. Fox, but however this may be, the fact of its being established so soon afterwards is sufficient for my purpose; as the measures that were proper at that conjuncture ought then to have been pursued, by which means the war might have terminated honourably, and perhaps with some compensation, certainly without loss and disgrace to Britain.

The course of the winds in the West-Indies being regularly directed from east to west, and without any, or with an ineffectual, variation, it follows that where the position of the islands is in the same direction, the descent from island to island is most expeditious; while the ascent is very laborious, and not to be effected but with a continual struggle, and by a most

F tedious

tedious navigation. Nor unless vessels are in good condition and excellent sailors, can it be attempted if at all, if the distance is considerable. Now St. Domingo with respect to the agregate of the Windward Islands, among which are to be counted also what are called the Leeward Islands which are windward in this respect, is precisely in this direction; so that the descent to St. Domingo is most expeditious, and is even the course pursued by vessels bound thither from Europe, which commonly make the Windward Islands in their passage, while the ascent from thence, particularly from the French part, is scarcely heard of; certain it is that an equipment from Europe would be more easily made, and more expeditious in its arrival. The defeat of Mr. de Grasse was in effect a double defeat. It was a defeat by sea, and it was a defeat by land. *Almost all the garrisons, as was notorious, were withdrawn from the French windward colonies, and embarked in the ships of war, for the purpose of attacking Jamaica

* The delightful and important colony of Guadaloupe had only a very few companies of a colonial regiment left in it.

with

with an accumulated force. But when this fleet was defeated and driven down to St. Domingo thefe troops were as far removed from what might have been a moft fruitful fcene of action; as if they had blown by fome tornado to Europe; as if new equipments were to have been made; as if new dangers were to be encountered in traverfing the feas, and a certainty of defeat or capture when they arrived at a blockaded port. In America an armiftice had been concluded: the tranfports were ready, though the Germans could not embark, the Britifh were eager, the paffage was fhort, the prize was rich, the fuccefs not doubtful; revenge and compenfation perfuaded, and fortune invited the enterprife. Did the Shelburne, which had now eftablifhed itfelf upon the ruins and difunion of the Rockingham adminiftration, take any advantage of this conjuncture fcarcely to be hoped, certainly not to be paralleled? Did the fplendid genius of the new Chancellor of the Exchequer illuminate with a ray of light the darknefs of the cabinet? By what fatal lethargy were their fenfes oppreffed? Or, when they found the defigns which public

fagacity

sagacity had imputed to them, and public virtue had frustrated, could not be carried into execution, did they revenge the safety of the nation by a malicious neglect of its interests?

For my part when I revolve all these things in my mind; when I consider that train of events that for some time back has been passing before us, and now continue to pass,—the disagreements of commanders—the surrender of armies—the conquests of Islands—the separation of a continent—the nations of the earth combined against one—the disunion of ministers—the insensibility and neglect of good fortune—despair cherished when hope might be indulged;—when I add to these a peace ingloriously concluded—equivalents not stipulated for cessions—attachment abandoned or requited by means subversive of industry, and fatal to morals, and the evil not even now expended,—I cannot help comparing in their manner of operating, the moral with the physical world; in which we find that in plants or animals, if any taint has been received and incorporated, a vicious nature is propagated; and it requires many descents, many commixtures, much time, much gradual alteration,

by

by addition, by diminution, by compofition, by change of relations of parts, before the taint is removed, and nature reftored: thus in the moral world, whatever caufes are laid, a kind of nature is propagated in the effects of thofe caufes, fo that after much time, after many removes, and a long defcent, a vicious conftitution fhall yet be traced in an extreme event, and the thread of evil drawn out through the more meafurelefs diftance*.

It

---

* It is hardly neceffary to ftate that the provifion for the Loyalifts is apropriated from the profits of an annual lottery; which is an evil not in itfelf, but inafmuch as it gives rife to the practife and furnifhes means to the rage of infuring; a rage that is as violent as it is abfurd and peculiarly fatal to the poor and ignorant.

The thefts, the proftitution, the drunkennefs, the defpair, the fuicide, which are neceffary effects of lofs and diftrefs, in fome natures; are all a part of the fame fyftem of events with the American war itfelf, as without that war the circumftance would not have happened, by which lotteries have become a part of annual ways and means; infurance is the effect of lotteries, and lofs and diftrefs a neceffary effect, as might be proved of infuring to an inconvenient amount. With refpect to all events being neceffary, I would refer my reader to Mr. Collins's Enquiry concerning Liberty:

and

It was not probable that an adminiftration whofe inaction was guilt, and whofe action was difgrace, fhould long fuftain itfelf againft the voice of reafon, of pride, and of indignation. A vote of cenfure was carried in the Houfe of Commons againft the terms of peace, which were declared inadequate; nor could the perpetrators of that meafure entertain any reafonable hope of extending their public exiftence under fo much infamy. Yet was not the game quite given up: for a game it was. The Marquis of Lanfdown, indeed late Earl of Shelburne, refigned; but Mr. Pitt, with a prophetic pertinacioufnefs, ftill retained his office of Chancellor of the Exchequer; it was even rumoured, poffibly it might have been propofed, that he fhould fucceed the Earl of Shelburne, as if the nation would receive fuch a fubftitution for an atonement, and the refignation of one minifter could expiate a guilty fyftem. In this fituation did

---

and it is with pleafure that I announce to the public, that a very ingenious and learned friend of mine propofes to republifh that fcarce and invaluable tract, with the addition of a preface, and fome account of the author, Mr. Collins, who was a profound and ingenious fearcher after truth, and an excellent man.

the

the nation continue for full five weeks, without any oftenfible minifter, without any effective government, in a crifis of peculiar difficulty and diftrefs, when a war was juft concluded, when the treafury was empty, when engagements were preffing, when taxes were not productive, when credit was low, when a loan was wanted, and a general alarm had diffufed itfelf over all ranks of people. His Majefty, however, at length, with a paternal folicitude, was gracioufly pleafed to condefcend to attend to the importunity of parliament, and to appoint an effective adminiftration.

This new adminiftration, which took place in the middle of the feffion of 1783, was formed by a coalition of parties; and Mr. Fox, whofe oppofition had been long and bitter, and fatal to the adminiftration of Lord North, was now feen to act amicably and jointly with him in the affairs of government: An event that made much noife at the time when it happened; that has been productive of a very extraordinary revolution, in the public opinion with refpect to one of the parties, has been attended with fome diminution of private efteem, with refpect to the other, and has been

been in its confequences extremely injurious to both. A great diftance of time has now intervened; furprize or aftonifhment no longer impedes the operations of judgment; even prejudice has abated of its malignity, and does not reject, though it, fufpicioufly, hears the voice of reafon and of impartial difcuffion; if therefore at a juncture fo feafonable, I fhall treat rather diffufely concerning that interefting event, I hope I fhall not be deemed impertinent, or I fhall receive indulgence.

In difcuffing the propriety of any meafure, or part of conduct, there is no other way of appreciating its merits, or of afcertaining its defects or its pravity, but by mounting up to fome general principle, and then, by confidering that meafure or part of conduct, relatively to fuch general principle: and the reafon why men form oppofite judgments concerning the fame actions, is, becaufe inftead of purfuing that courfe, and referring to an immutable ftandard, each man forms a ftandard of his own, adapted to his prejudices, his intereft, or his habits, which is, therefore, not only neceffarily different in different men; but even varies in the fame man, according to the changes

changes that may happen in any of the aforementioned circumstances; a truth that we have probably all of us experienced, if only we had the candour to acknowledge it.

That wisdom consists in adapting means to the end proposed; is a position not to be disputed: and as wisdom will not propose any but a virtuous end, so the acceptation of this principle thus defined, will not only not pervert conduct, but will even be the proper standard of its beauty or deformity. Wisdom is conversant with all the actions of life, which as they are not less different in their nature than in their object or design, so must the means that are used in obtaining such different objects, be essentially different, so that what would be the effect of consummate wisdom in one case, would, in the other, be the effect of consummate folly. Now, the duties of man, I speak of civilized, social man, are twofold: first, there is a duty that he owes to himself; which may be called the selfish duty. This duty or principle, is an immediate derivation from nature, and is particular and limited in its operation. Secondly, there is a duty that he owes to the community, of which he is a member;

and this latter duty which is the immediate effect of reflection, though it may be traced ultimately to nature, is general and univerſal in its operation. It appears then, that there is an eſſential difference between the objects of theſe two duties, one of which I have called the ſelfiſh, and the other I call the ſocial, and indeed this is ſo much the caſe, that any great prevalency of the one, is abſolutely inconſiſtent with the very exiſtence of the other, prudence claiming an equipoiſe of both; but generous virtue not ſeldom forfeiting her reward by the prevalency of the latter, which, as its object is neceſſarily general, while the object of the former is neceſſarily particular; ſo are the means it uſes much more enlarged and proportionate its greater ſcale of action.

If this diſtinction is juſt, it follows that where the public is concerned, a different meaſure of action is abſolutely required from that which would be approved of, if only the individual were concerned. Let me endeavour to give this matter a little illuſtration. In the intercourſe of private life, friendſhip and enmity, benevolence and reſentment, are permited to mingle; and the paſſions, yet under ſubordination,

ordination, declare themselves with approbation, when the individual alone is concerned. In the heart, that is warm, nor artifice, nor simulation, nor treachery, nor malignity have any place, and though the individual is betrayed into indiscretions, and may suffer inconveniencies, yet is the general security connected with the particular evil, and what conduces to public utility the consent of all will approve. But it is no less certain that the interposition of the passions in conduct, is immediately connected with the selfish principle: We can neither love nor hate, we cannot confer a kindness, nor entertain resentment without indulging a propensity, and gratifying our nature. If in doing this we have abandoned an interest, we have yet enjoyed a pleasure, which we thought, upon the whole, it was better for us to enjoy, even upon what might be thought disadvantageous terms, if it were weighed in the scale of what is called worldly prudence. And this conduct will not only be approved of, but even demanded; because the principle is useful, and the inconvenience which may and most commonly does result, being particular, the public will not confider the event, but only the general tendency of the principle, and the fecurity that it propofes.

But in refpect of that *fyftem* of conduct, whereof the individual is only the inftrument, and the event of which applies directly to the community at large; the cafe is widely different, and indeed diametrically oppofite: When we forego a private intereft for the gratification of a paffion, a compenfation of pleafure has been received for the facrifice of an advantage; a compenfation that is greater than the facrifice; for if it were not, we fhould, undoubtedly, forego the pleafure, and purfue the advantage, which would then be the compenfation, fince it is not in our power to enjoy both; one being the price of the other.

But if you allow the paffions to mingle in public conduct; if, without confidering the nature of the conjuncture, and what ought to be the determination of action relatively to that conjuncture, fo as that the greateft benefit fhould arife from it; you fhould fay, " This " man has kept me long in a fruitlefs oppo- " fition; I have condemned his meafures; I hate

"I hate his perfon; whatever interefts I may
"fuffer, I will gratify my refentment; and
"though there is now no fubject of difagree-
"ment, I will not unite." What is this in
fact but to make a property of the public,
and to facrifice the general interefts to your
own? Whatever courfe of conduct you purfue, you purfue it becaufe your interefts are
concerned: and when you facrifice your advantage to your refentment, you have ftill
purfued your interefts, not indeed rightly underftood; and you have your compenfation
becaufe you think you have it. But does the
public enjoy any part of this compenfation?
Does your perfonal gratification diffufe itfelf
through all the ranks and orders of men of
which the community is compofed? Are
your feelings the meafure of their feelings?
Your good the meafure of their good? Your
exiftence the meafure of their exiftence?

Vain and foolifh thought! Know, that
every bird that flies in the air, every beaft that
treads, every reptile that creeps upon the fur-
face or hides itfelf in the bofom of the earth,
and perhaps every part and particle of nature,
has each a fyftem of his own, feparate and

diftinct

diſtinct from, though externally related to, all other ſyſtems. Like man himſelf who aſſerts his proud ſuperiority, each has its intereſts to purſue, accommodated to its exiſtence; each its paſſions to gratify: reſentment, friendſhip, love, hatred, deſire, antipathy, ſympathy, are theirs. In what then does the excellence of man conſiſt? It conſiſts in this; that he has the power to break the priſon gates of his particular exiſtence, to expand in general contemplations, to ſend forth his thoughts to diſcover the relations of things, their fitneſs, their diſpoſition to produce good under every poſſible combination; it conſiſts in the power to abſtract qualities from ſubſtances, and capacities from the groſs objects in which they where, and by paſſing over whatever is particular and perſonal, to leave no room for prejudice or favour, or the paſſions to diſturb the judgment, or render ineffectual the great object of his ſublime inquiries. It is then only by ſuch enlarged contemplations, it is by abſtracting qualities and capacities, and uſing them without any perſonal regards, when the conjuncture requires it, that general good

can

can be effected or secured. Whether we love or whether we hate, if these are necessary to the service of the community, of which each one is a part, and a no greater part than the meanest individual, there is an equal obligation to employ them, and any distinction in such a case would be vain and wicked.

But you will say, demonstrate as much as you please, the virtuous efficacy of these sublime abstractions of qualities and capacities from persons, have you yet shewn that it is practicable to do it? Are we not conscious that the weakness of mankind is affected principally by sensible objects, and that even the knife which divides the skin and causes pain, though it is not an agent, is sometimes thrown away with precipitation, and its very sight becomes offensive. How then shall we be able not to hate the person whose measures, though at a time past, have been obnoxious, and the subject of a bitter and continued opposition, and hating the person; by what moral chemistry shall we separate his qualities and capacities, and employ them in the strictest union with our own, though it should be for the public service?

To

To this I answer. First, in general that if the propriety of such abstractions, arising from the nature of our public duty, which I have shewn, is essentially different from our private duty; one having the part without any regard to the whole, and the other the whole without any regard to the part, for its object, has been in any wise demonstrated; the possibility of them is demonstrated by that very truth: for a bountiful Providence has so adapted human capacity to human ends, that whatever is our duty, is possible, and not only possible, but easy also. Secondly, I say that this very weakness of mankind, which causes us to be affected so strongly by sensible objects, is an argument that answers as well my purpose as that of my adversaries, and is equally conclusive in either case: for when the measures that have occasioned opposition and personal hatred, if, we admit, the very illiberal position that these things are necessarily connected, have ceased to be; and a conformity of views of interest and of conduct has taken place; the same proneness to be affected by sense, which had before operated as a cause of enmity, will now operate as a cause of friendship;

ſhip; that very circumſtance which is dogmatically ſtated as an argument why enmity ſhould be perpetual, will occaſion the engagements of friendſhip, and theſe notable reaſoners will diſcover that they have argued from a conſequence as it was a cauſe, and have confounded a general principle with a particular fact.

The amount of my theory upon this occaſion is, though that whenever the dilemma ſhould be between the public ſervice and private feelings, the nature of our public duty requires the ſacrifice of private feelings to the public ſervice: that whenever the dilemma ſhould be between private intereſt and private feelings, the nature of our private duty, which may be defined, a ſenſe of dignity, for without dignity there can be no virtue, juſtifies and even demands a ſacrifice of private intereſt; nor is the ſelfiſh principle affected by this conduct, ſince, in the indulgence of feelings, a compenſation is received for the ſacrifice of intereſt, which is in no wiſe the caſe with reſpect to public tranſactions, the public being a party to the loſs, but no party to the compenſation; and I deduce from hence, that it is the confusion of these duties which occasions the wrong judgments that are formed concerning their means, and has been the cause of all that clamour against the union of Lord North and Mr. Fox, or as it is invidiously termed, the coalition, but which, if we try it by the test of circumstances, admitting the principles I have laid down to be just, we shall find to be not only defensible, but meritorious and honourable.

To suppose that every measure which is submitted to Parliament receives a judgment upon its own merits, that there a total absence of favour, or of prejudice, no habitual concurrence nor opposition, that there is no bias from hopes frustrated, from views entertained, from personal, from public motives, from ill success, from misconduct, from imputed treachery, from national loss, or disgrace— were to suppose a state of indifferency in men's minds, which will be no where experienced, but least of all in a popular assembly. The consequence of this condition of things is, that where several parties are formed in such a body, with opposite views, prejudices, and impressions, and these parties are nearly balanced in power

power and authority; it is impossible that there should be any administration, or any government, without a union of some of them, and a total oblivion of former animosities. Such was the state of parties, and such the necessity of a junction, at the close of last war. There were three parties in Parliament adhering to different leaders. A single one of these could not retain or assume the reins of government, for it was certain to sink under the superiority of the other two which would unite for its destruction: it was then a matter not of choice but of necessity, that two of them should unite in order to give stability to government, and effect to its measures. But how, or by which of these parties was such a union to be formed? Could either of these that was out, unite with that which was in? But they had both agreed in stigmatizing the conduct of an administration, which they declared had sacrificed the interests, and abandoned the honour, of the country by an inadequate and inglorious peace. Could either of these embrace in the very midst of its reproaches, and without any atonement from example, such a party? Could it say in the same breath, " Your
" terms

"terms of peace are inadequate, you have "diſhonoured, you have diſgraced us: you "have forfeited our confidence; but take "us in, we will yet maintain you, only we will "divide the gains." Should they not rather ſay to each other, "We have diſagreed upon "former points, but we have ſince that fought "the ſame battle; we have united without "blame to expel an adminiſtration, ſhall any "blame attach if we unite to form one?" A union which is not condemned in one caſe ſurely may be approved in the other. Such would be the language of reaſon, and ſuch was the conduct of Mr. Fox and Lord North in this memorable conjuncture.

There were moreover ſome circumſtances attending the compoſition of this adminiſtration which has been the object of general reproach, peculiarly agreeable to moderate and diſcerning men: (and ſo different are the judgments that people form upon the ſame ſubject,) the very cauſes of diſguſt and horror in others, viz. the difference in the principles upon certain great queſtions of the two leading men in it, were to them occaſions of ſatisfaction and pledges of ſecurity. It rarely hap-
hens

pens that our opinions agree precisely upon a theory so nice as that of government in its most simple forms. But in a government so blended as the British, the disagreement is the more likely to happen in respect of the greater variety and complication of interests, and the adjustment and balance of power of each branch, by the concurrence of all of which, and by the influence of each upon either, the government is constituted. To suppose that the frame of the British Constitution is better calculated for duration in an unchangeable state than any other more simple form of government, is an error which I shall take some pains to discuss in its proper place. The truth is, that there is no such thing as existence of any kind, whether of natural bodies, or of human institutions, without a contention of parts; nor can there be a contention of parts without an alteration or change in the powers of those parts. How far an ascendancy has been obtained by any one, or by which of the parts of the British constitution, I shall leave it to the impartial historian, from a consideration of the measures and of the events of his majesty's reign, to determine. But this

is

is not yet to our purpose. Now, that which determines the course of government, in its future progress, whether to a more popular, to a more aristocratical, or to a more regal form, is the adoption or rejection of certain acts, such as are conversant with general policy; and do not relate to particular measures arising from conjunctures, in which the action, and consequently the union, of ministers is absolutely necessary. And as the former are questions that do not impede the course of administration, let them be decided which way they may, so ministers who do not entertain the same sentiments upon them, do not only not unite but even debate and divide against each other whenever they are agitated, and the public business is not affected. It appears then that admitting the fact, that things should remain as they are, a diversity of sentiment among ministers openly professed and steadily maintained, is extremely to be desired, inasmuch as it is the best security against innovation, for the influence which ministers necessarily have being divided upon such occasions, there can be little danger of success to such

such an attempt from ministerial influence. On the other hand, if things should not remain as they are, and innovation should be deemed proper for the sake of renovation, this division of influence, at the same time that it might tend to introduce moderation, would not prevent a reform; for the votes of ministers dividing against each other, and the scales being nearly equal, a preponderancy would be secured in favour of public good, by those honest independent men, (and doubtless many such there are,) who being creatures of no party, influenced by no motives of private advantage, addicted to no authority, are able to exercise their pure, unbiassed, unprejudiced reason in the execution of their most important trust.

From such an administration then as the Coalition, a character of temper and moderation, and an assurance of perfect security to the present state of the constitution, or of its rational improvement, was most certainly to be expected by all men of discernment; who did not take words for things, and who deemed that coalition the proper object of their disgust and horror, whereby they saw Mr. Pitt

Pitt linked in the clofeft bonds of union with Mr. Jenkinfon, a name which has always been connected in public opinion, how juftly I know not, with fecret influence, with a clandeftine government, and with all the feries of difgrace and calamity which had fo long affected this unhappy country.

Thefe men judged, and they judged from a knowledge of the human heart, that the old fyftem, if any fuch there were, might fome day be revived with a double energy by fuch a union: that a fplendid name, that popular beginnings, talents, which aftonifhed by their early maturity, co-operating with the difguft that was conceived againft the other coalition, might render Mr. Pitt a convenient oftenfible Minifter in the hands of fecret advifers, and of a dark cabal; and that the public, dazzled by the blaze which furrounded the inftrument of Government, would no longer fee the means which before, it thought at leaft that it clearly, difcerned, and exceffive light would produce a fatal obfcurity.

But whatever might have been the clamour of people without doors, and the difcontent of fome few within, the coalition adminiftration,

tion, by taking in whatever of ability there was in all parties, and profcribing none, though fome voluntarily excluded themfelves, was both very ftrong and very well calculated by the uncommon unafumity that it infpired, for the very critical conjuncture, in which it conducted the affairs of government. During the remainder of the feffion, fo fugitive is power that depends only upon the patronage of office, thofe who were fo lately minifters, and now the oppofition, fcarcely dared to promulgate their weaknefs by a divifion; and whatever was propofed was carried almoft without a cavil, if you except fome few objections that were made to the terms of the loan; the bargain for which was precipitated, and an advantage taken of the great and increafed preffure of the public exigency, arifing from the continuance of the former Chancellor of the Exchequer, in office, when his powers of action were extinguifhed, and during the time when the loan ought to have been negotiated.

The next feffion of Parliament, 1783—84, will be always memorable in the annals of this country, from the events it gave birth to, from the extraordinary revolution it perfected in men's minds, a revolution that had began to operate from the date of the coalition, and from all the abfurdities which grew from that fruitful parent; but above all, it will be memorable from the unparalleled circumftance of a Minifter retaining his fituation, in defiance of the efforts to difplace him, of a majority in parliament; avowing himfelf the Minifter of the Crown againft the fenfe of the people, and yet retaining his popularity, and finally eftablifhing himfelf, by the very means, when they turned in his favour, which he had refifted and defied, without any imputation of inconfiftency in his principles or in his conduct.

But yet if we turn a philofophic eye upon this jumble of events, which feem to fet human reafon at naught in its attempts to account for them from any fixed principles; if we confider the over-grown influence of the minifter of the crown arifing from a boundlefs patronage, and a dangering empire over the hopes of man; the weight of great public bodies, and of vaft maffes of private wealth acting in concert, and under difcipline,

to

to obtain a given purpose; and, in fine, the prevalency of folly over wisdom, of error over truth;—we shall not be more surprised at this part of our history, nor shall we deem it a more extraordinary picture of human absurdity, than has before occurred in the history of our own, and of other, nations; in which we may generally observe, that the quantum of error may be measured by the quantum of violence of those who entertain it, and of the conviction with which they seem to be impressed of the truth and justice of their opinion.

The fame that Mr. Fox had acquired by a splendid display of talents upon all occasions, during a long course of Parliamentary services, commenced at a very early period of life, and continued without intermission; had raised very high the expectations of all men concerning the issue of the day on which he was to open his plan for the better government of India: It is not more than justice to add, that his atchievement on that and the succeeding days in which his bill was debated, exceeded the expectations of all men. The bill met with a most violent opposition.

It was argued, that the taking the whole conduct of Indian affairs, civil, political, and commercial, from the courts of directors and of proprietors, and vesting them in certain commissioners to be appointed by Parliament, for a certain term of years, was a most indecent and outrageous violation of a solemn compact that Government, for a valuable consideration, had made and ratified with the East-India Company.

That by the charter of the company, the whole management of their affairs was vested in the said bodies with competent powers and authorities; but to substitute another species of government, was a direct invasion of these charters; nor did the evil rest here, for that the same consequences might be extended to the other charters of the kingdom, and the insecurity of all was established by the fate of one. That such violence was justly to be compared with that which was exercised in the dangerous reign of Charles II. when, on account of its virtuous opposition to the Court, the City of London was deprived of its corporate rights; nor did the other corporations in the kingdom escape the common ruin;

ruin; and their charters being taken away or garbled, left the liberties of the people entirely at the mercy of the crown, by setting up a fatal power in that branch, of mutilating the representative body, or of imposing its own conditions upon the rights of election. That no necessity for so strong a measure had yet been proved; and when means less violent would serve, it was not only impolitic to pursue violent ones, but such conduct was a strong presumption of some wicked design, which did not yet appear. Such steps then, not having any commensurate object, should awaken suspicion, and excite alarm. That vesting the Indian affairs in Commissioners, to be appointed by Parliament, must have one of two objects in view (for it was thus variously argued). It must increase the influence of the crown by giving it the Indian, in addition to its other patronage already too great; or, it must diminish the influence of the crown, by setting up a patronage in individuals, which ought, according to the legal course of the constitution, to be vested only in the crown, and rendering ministers quite independent of that branch of the government.

Finally,

Finally, that it would eftablifh a fourth power in the ftate, an imperium in imperio. A monfter in any government that admits it.

On the other hand it was argued by thofe who fupported the bill, that by the charter of the Eaft-India Company, a right of Government had been vefted in that body; but it was a right of governing well; a right of governing ill, no power could beftow.

That all government was revocable for abufe; a principle not only juft in theory, but recognized by the *practice* of the Britifh conftitution. The fact then of the bad government of the India Company being admitted, as all the reports on the table were full of the ufurpations, the rapine, the treachery of the Company's fervants abroad; of countries defolated, of princes dethroned, of nations extirpated, facred prejudices violated, and neither age, nor fex, nor condition, nor fanctity fpared by unholy violence, and the perpetrators of thefe acts not cenfured, not recalled, not punifhed by their mafters, but applauded and maintained for the fruit of their crimes—the taking the government out of fuch hands, and vefting it elfewhere, was a matter of urgent neceffity necessity and not of choice or deliberation. That no palliative could correct the evil; the constitution of government under the charter being radically bad. That the Courts of Directors and Proprietors were not the masters, they were the instruments of their pretended servants, or they were bribed by the participation of the plunder, in an increased dividend, to acquiesce in crimes at which their distance from the scene where they were perpetrated, did not allow the sensibility of their nature to revolt. That if it was necessary to substitute another species of government for Indian affairs to this vicious one, could it be so well placed as under the immediate control and inspection of Parliament, in responsible persons, and in a public execution of duty. That should some objections be started even against this mode, yet as wisdom consisted not in rejecting measures, because in some respects defective, and suffering the worse to take its course, but in selecting among different measures, such as were the least objectionable; if it could be proved that the mode now proposed was better than any other, the framers of it should have credit for the good, and the

evil

evil should be referred to the nature and constitution of things. It was asked, where should the government of Indian affairs be vested? Should it be vested without condition, or stint in the crown? This would be to increase an influence already too great. Should it be left where it was? This would be to perpetuate the horrors complained of. What too were the objections to the principle of this bill? That it increased, that it diminished the influence of the crown; that it established another power in the state. Against these it was urged that the two first objections, like affimative and negative quantities, destroyed each other; neither could be very evident, or both would not be entertained; that with respect to the latter in particular, which was sustained upon this ground, viz. " that it gave an unconstitutional influence to " the persons of the ministers, by the appointment of their friends to the commission:" the reasoning was fallacious and unfair, it was deserting a principle, and arguing from an abuse, which might, or might not exist; that a parliamentary act was to be understood to be completely such, and not an

act

act of perfonal favour. That to extend this mode of arguing would be to diffolve all government, and to render the interpretation of every meafure particular and capricious, inftead of being general and ftable. That with refpect to the laft objection of its eftablifhing an imperium in imperio, it was an affertion, and not an argument, and an affertion adapted only to vulgar capacities to make or to receive. That if any fuch thing could exift, it exifted in its worft effects in the prefent government of the India Company, thofe then who made this clamour, and denied at the fame time that parliament fhould interfere, or wifhed to limit that interference with a groffnefs of intellect fcarcely to be conceived, gave the lie to the object of their own argument by fupporting a power independant, or in the greates and poffible independance of the fupreme power of the ftate.

Which party was right upon this very important occafion, it is not for me to decide, the public has already decreed; perhaps the day is not far removed, when the fame public, from a fatal experience of the effects flowing from a different fyftem, fhall reverfe that decree with grief and repentance. The bill, however, passed the Commons by a very great majority; but being sent to the Lords its progress was at first impeded by artificial delays, and it was at length finally rejected in that house.

The means that were used to procure the rejection of the India Bill in the Lords, the secret machinations, the midnight conspiracies, the insinuations, the whispers, the threats, the effect of these upon the conduct of some noble lords, who promised and withdrew their support almost in the same breath, and yielded to influence what honour should have maintained; are not touched upon here, or are slightly touched upon for the sake of preserving the thread of history. The author suppresses truth to avoid a libel.

Presently after this event, on the 18th of December, at twelve o'clock at night, the seals were demanded from the two Secretaries of State, who were dismissed from their offices. A resignation of all the other members of the the cabinet immediately took place; and the appointment of Mr. Pitt to the offices of first Lord of the Treasury and Chancellor of the Exchequer

Exchequer was announced to the public, together with an entire new administration.

We have now arrived at that period of our history which contains one of the most extraordinary political dilemmas that has ever yet, or as it is sincerely to be hoped, ever will be again experienced by this nation. There was seen at the same moment a minister, calling himself minister of the crown, and yet born up by a tide of popularity, such as had never flowed with more violence in its natural direction; there was seen, for the ample space of more than three months, a contention between prerogative and privilege; a minister maintaining his place, and yet denied to act; a House of Commons refusing every confidence to a minister and yet obliged to submit to his continuance in office; the fatal consequences that might arise from such a state of things disregarded, and finally a triumph of rashness over moderation, and a voluntary desertion on the part of the people of that body which is constituted to protect their rights, and which they could not abandon upon such an occasion without establishing the fatal conclusion that their own consent was not necessary to the continuance in office of a minister, or that if it was necessary, the House of Commons was not at every period of its existence the representative of the nation and the organ of its will. The first of these consequences we should find dangerous to liberty, as it amounts to little less than an acknowledgment, if we trace its effects, of arbitrary power in the crown; the second could not fail to produce all the anarchy and confusion which must flow from the dissolution, or the supposed dissolution, at any time, of legal government.

But as this matter involves a constitutional question of no small importance it deserves some discussion; let us enquire without passion, and let us judge with candour. In every civilized country a form of government of some kind is established; and whether it is simple or whether it is complex, whether it is a pure monarchy, a pure aristocracy, or a pure democracy, or whether it is mixed or compounded of all, or of any of these, such a government or constitution is binding upon the people, and they must accept of all its consequences, so long at least as they think their form a good one, and are willing not to change it.

Now

Now the Government of Great Britain is compofed of King, Lords, and Commons, and its beauty and efficacy is fuppofed to confift in very nice balances, fo that one fhall not ufurp upon another, for the prevention of which each is armed with a negative; for experience informs us, and if it did not, our reafoning a priori from the nature of man would inform us, that there is nothing which the human bofom fo fondly defires, or fo ardently purfues as the poffeffion of power, as there is then in thefe feveral branches, a diftinct intereft, fo is there in each a principle of ufurpation, which is precifely commenfurate with the means that it has of executing its purpofe, and the greatnefs of the benefit that will accure to either upon the attainment of what it aims at.

In a country that is very large and very populous, and where the government is democratical, or in part democratical, fuch as it is in Great Britain and Ireland, the people never can be called upon collectively to take their fhare in public affairs. They can only do this virtually, that is by the election of certain delegates or reprefentatives, of a number not

too

too large to assemble and deliberate, and not so small as to lose the character of popularity. And these representatives must be intrusted for the term of their duration with powers very ample, for less would not be sufficient for the purpose of legislation, which is the highest act of authority that men can exercise.

In the contemplation of such a constitution, so soon as the representative begins to exist, the political existence of the elective body entirely ceases, and the voice of the people is as completely expressed within the walls of the House of Commons, as if it was delivered from the collected multitude upon some boundless plain.

This is the theory of our constitution: I am very far from saying that the case is in fact such as I have stated it to be; that it is not so—is an abuse; but while we preserve the frame precisely as it is, we must take all its consequences generally, for all are essential to the existence of the identical frame. It appears then from this statement, that a question between the crown and commons, if we admit of the principle of representation, without

out which our form of government cannot subsist at all, must be a question between the crown and the people: The commons and the people, constitutionally considered, being the very same thing.

Now if a question were proposed, thus: Has the crown a right to maintain a minister against the inclination, and against the requisition of a majority of the people of England, supposing the people could be assembled, and such majority ascertained? I should be glad to know what hardy stickler for prerogative would think it prudent to exercise such a right; and a right that ought not to be exercised is no right all; and if the crown could not exercise such a right in opposition to the whole people of England, but can exercise it in opposition to the requisition of the House of Commons? My next question would be, Does the House of Commons represent the people? If it does, how will you distinguish those that represent, from those who are represented? Surely, you cannot do it; you might as well distinguish a guinea from twenty one shillings, whereof the value is the same, the appearance only is different. If it does

does not reprefent the people, then is the boafted form of government of Great-Britain, in that part where, with all its defects, it may be deemed by many to be the moft unexceptionable, merely nominal and a mockery, and the people have been deluded for ages, with the appearances of freedom, when they have been the mere tools and inftruments of their own fervitude, the hewers of wood and the drawers of water to unmerciful tafk-mafters.

But it is argued that in the particular cafe, the Houfe of Commons did not exprefs the wifhes of the people, but the reverfe as appeared very plainly from the fubfequent events upon an appeal to the people, and confequently in the particular cafe; quoad hoc, the reprefentation was incomplete, and the Houfe of Commons, and the people, were not identical. Now fuch an argument amounts to this: viz. that the Houfe fometimes does reprefent, and fometimes does not reprefent, the people. Shall I anfwer this ferioufly? certainly, no; I will not infult my reader. I remember a ftory that was popular at College of a young man, who being examined previoufly to the taking his degrees, was afked,

Whether

Whether the sun moved round the earth, or the earth round the sun? The question was a difficult one, and how should it be answered at once? it was better to be partly right, than entirely wrong, for prudence is more nearly allied to ignorance than is generally suspected; and so after some time spent in considering, the answer, and truly a most notable one, was " Sometimes the one, and sometimes the other." Now I do shrewdly suspect that this same gentleman is one of the political reasoners who do so much honour to the present administration, Agnosco stylum, and who argue that the House of Commons sometimes does represent, and sometimes does not represent, the people: that is to say, while there is a majority in favour of the minister of the crown, and the parliament is quite implicit and obedient, the representation is perfect; but if it becomes rebellious at any time, for instance, if it had done so upon this late occasion of the Russian war, then the representation would cease to be perfect; and if in such a case as happened in a former one, the corporations which return so large a portion of members, could be persuaded that the safety of their charters was connected with supporting the minister of the crown, against the privileges of the people; there is no doubt but a dissolution would be attended with the same salutary effects; and a new parliament being purged of every thing that was refractory, would leave the minister to prosecute the Russian, or any other war, the causes of which the sanctity of his Majesty's councils would not endure, that profane curiosity should enquire into.

In truth, the character, the objects, the duties of public bodies are founded in unchangeable relations: so that if we maintain that the House of Commons is the representative of the people at any time, we must maintain that it is so at all times; if we deny that it is so at any time, we must deny that it is so at all times; while its constitution remains the same; we must deny the legitimacy of that branch of the government which is the pride, the boast, and the only security of Englishmen. That parliament then, which was insulted by the minister of the crown, and deserted by the people, was entitled to the same support from the people, that the last parliament was, or the present is, or any future one

one will be; nor did Mr. Pitt, when he maintained his situation of minister in defiance of the voice of that House, less violate a general principle of the constitution; nor did he less degrade the popular part of the government, or establish a less dangerous precedent, than if he had maintained it in defiance of the voice itself of a majority of the people of England, or if he were to maintain it in defiance of the voice of the present, or of any future parliament: for although the composition of this body is made up of fleeting parts that pass away, and are succeeded in the changes which gross matter is subject to, so that in one session it does not consist of the same, that it did in a former, or will do in a future session; and one parliament is not composed of the identical members that a former was, or a future parliament will be; as the gross substance of the human body is supposed to be entirely changed, so that at the end of seven years, not one particle of it shall remain in the same person; thus, though men may succeed men in one or in different parliaments, yet the body itself continues to exist; nor can, identity, be ever destroyed, where the spirit is immortal:

tal: and whatever indignity or infult, or injury has been at any time received, it remains indelibly infixed to future times and to future ages; not to be expiated, but by a folemn acknowledgement of the offence, and a punifhment or cenfure of the guilty offender.

In judging, therefore, of the conduct of the minifter upon this memorable occafion, we muft abandon the particular fact, and we muft refort to the general principle. If a minifter, calling himfelf minifter of the crown, could wage open war with the reprefentatives of the people, even with the fuppofed confent and approbation of the people, if he could maintain his fituation in defiance of every effort to remove him, if he could elude their applications upon points of the neareft concern by evafions that are always difhoneft, or infult their feelings by contemptuous filence —then is the fatal precedent fet, and the Houfe of Commons muft ever after be deemed of the fmalleft importance, or rather quite infignificant in the fcale of government, for the fame conduct may be ufed to future parliaments, upon fimilar prefumptions, and the authority of every one is diminifhed, and its condition degraded,

graded, by the same act; and if you should be startled at such a consequence, as I trust every lover of his country, and every friend to liberty must be, but should argue that the House deserved the severe infliction from its own misconduct on the particular occasion; I would just suggest, that a judgment concerning any particular fact, is only a matter of opinion, which is generally different in different men; but even admitting that all men agreed in a condemnation of it, yet when a general principle, especially such a one as vitally affects a constitution of government, and a particular fact, are at variance so, as that different consequences must be drawn from either, there can be no proof so strong of human weakness, of human frailty, or of human depravity, as to make the general principle give way to the particular fact, and thus to abandon whatever is sacred in laws, in politics, and in the order of nature itself.

But should it be urged (turning my own datum, with which I set out, against me, viz. that where power was divided in different bodies or branches, there was a principle of usurpation in each, arising from the constitution

tion of man) that if at any time the Commons were to usurp upon the prerogative which the crown possesses, not indeed as a personal right, but as a trust for the good of the people; and therefore virtually a part of their privileges, would not a member of the House of Commons, admitting the fact that the majority wanted to innovate, act constitutionally, in avowing himself minister of the crown, in opposition to that majority, and in support indirectly indeed of the rights of the people with which the just prerogative of the crown is intimately connected. To this strong case (not that there is any kind of analogy between the case that has happened, and that which is now supposed, by way of argument, and to put this matter in the strongest point of view) I do not hesitate to answer NO. For that it is safer that a particular inconvenience should be suffered, than a general principle violated. While the House of Commons subsists, there is, according to the terms of the constitution, an inviolable connection between that House and the people: to resist a majority of the representatives of the people, is to resist a majority of the people; for I defy you, with any poli-
cal

tical chemiftry, to feparate them in theory; and if you feparate them in fact, the danger to be apprehended is too great for any particular advantage, in any poffible cafe to compenfate, fince nothing lefs than a diffolution of government may be expected, by extending this doctrine to a few more cafes, and particularly to fuch wherein the Crown and the Parliament agree, for the people will then have no other means of redrefs, than by refiftance and rebellion; and it is a fomewhat fingular fact in the hiftory of the prefent times, that in all the meafures in which Parliament has concurred with minifters, in all the wars they have engaged in, in the taxes they have impofed, in the armaments they have countenanced, in the confidence they have lavifhed, the union between the people and their reprefentatives has always been deemed complete, fo as that the acts of the legiflature could never be queftioned: but in the fingle inftance in which they have difagreed with a minifter, their fenfe has not only not been deemed the fenfe of the people, but being the ground of a violent proceeding, the event has juftified the meafure. A ftrong proof that the electors are

more

more corrupt than the elected, (since the latter, in the course of many years, have given at least one proof of independence) and that in the present state of the representation, the influence without doors is at least as great as it is within.

But you will ask what is to be done in the supposed case, that the Commons usurp upon either of the other branches of the constitution? is there no remedy? no preventive to be resorted to? and must a base acquiescence permit the evil to take its course, and the government to be over-turned? To this I answer, that in such a case the crown is armed with the power of dissolution—that House is no more—and the question is now indifferent to be decided, only by the sense of a future parliament. Does the King call you to his councils? obey the summons: there is no declaration against you: you do no violence to the popular branch of the government: you do not despise its authority: you do not degrade its condition: And, let me add, that after having resisted for more than three months the sense of the Commons, and their endeavours to remove you, when you at last
find

find your place untenable, and are obliged to resort to a diffolution, and the event of a general election, to fecure it: you give up the point in difpute, and you acknowledge that a minifter cannot, in fact, maintain his place without the confent of the Commons: for all the time then that you remained minifter againft fuch confent you violated a practical part of the conftitution; you criminate yourfelf by the very means that you take to efcape cenfure, and you ftand felf convicted, that you may elude the condemnation of others.

And, in God's name, what was the fact? and what were the extravagant demands of the Commons which caufed fo much madnefs in the nation at this celebrated juncture? they demanded that the miniftry fhould be perfons in whom they could repofe a confidence. In the tranfactions of private life, between two individuals, what is more common than for either party to object to an agent whom he thinks he cannot truft? and are the people of fo little account, fo bafe, fo contemptible, that they fhall not have the right of objecting, by the means of their only

only organ to the appointment of agents, in business that I had almost said was ALL THEIR OWN. Surely the people have such a right, if they have it not by the theory, they have it by the practise of the constitution; and any attempt to question or to subvert that right, in the representatives of the people, who must be so to all intents and purposes, if they are so at all. Whether it is made at this juncture, or whether it was made seven or ten years ago, or whatever particular circumstances it might have been attended with, deserves, not servile and interested panegyrick, not the effusions of gratitude, not triumphant success, but animadversion, and reproach, and defeat.

There is also another matter worthy of observation upon this subject, and this is, that with respect to any struggle between the Commons and the other branches of the legislature, it is not only, in general, an act of political suicide for the people to desert their representatives; but there is a reason to be derived from human nature, wherefore an impartial judge, and one who was not at all concerned in the event of the affray, would be extremely

extremely cautious, not only in taking it for granted, but even in determining upon apparent circumſtances, that reaſon and juſtice were not on the ſide of the Commons. For if it is true, from the moral conſtitution of mankind, which ſome have even confounded with the phyſical, that wherever power is diſtributed in different branches, each deſires to increaſe its ſhare, and obtain an aſcendant (and why this ſtruggle does not ſenſibly appear in our form of government, I ſhall endeavour to explain in the ſubſequent part of this ſketch) I ſay, if this is true, it is equally true that ſuch a principle is merely ſelfiſh; and would operate with the greateſt certainty and efficacy upon that branch, to which an apropriate conduct would produce the greateſt advantage. Now as the Houſe of Commons conſiſts of a greater number of individuals than any other branch of the government, and conſequently the power acquired by uſurpation upon the others, would be leſs to each member, and, beſides, as the tenure is uncertain, ſo as that he who is member to day, may not be ſo to-morrow; whereas in the other branches, the tenure is certain as to persons, and hereditary as to families; so from these combined causes, we may be pretty sure, reasoning from the nature of man, that a House of Commons will not, in general, be the aggressor; and if in such struggles it has sometimes forgot its moderation, and elate with victory, or smarting from the wounds it has received in the contest, or fearful of the future, from the experience of the past, it has pushed its advantage to an extreme length, such a conduct is the natural effect of human infirmity; nor does it carry with it any proof, or serve to discover which of the three branches the crime of unjust pretensions is originally to be imputed to.

In truth, the whole of this matter is so plain to the most ordinary understanding, that no minister could ever have expected, I do not say to acquire popularity, but to escape odium, by maintaining such a cause, if other circumstances had not occurred, by which the passions of the people were inflamed, and their reason disturbed by the furious access. One cause, among others of this delirium, was the supposed danger of Corporate Rights all over the kingdom, arising from the pretended vio-

lation

lation of the Charter of the East-India Company; and as every corporation, by a vanity which is inherent in men, was fond of claffing itfelf with a company, whofe poffeffions were kingdoms, and whofe authority was imperial; and exifting as they did by a charter, was derived from a common parent, and excited all the fympathy of confanguinity; fo the caufe immediately became a common one throughout the nation; nor is it wonderful that perfons living at a diftance from the fcene of action, for we find that the electors of Weftminfter were ftill true to their caufe, fhould be deluded by falfe ftatements; or even if they heard both fides of the queftion, that their pity fhould incline them in favour of the oppreft, while their fears fhould difpofe them againft the oppreffors.

But if they had only for a moment confidered how different the powers are which are granted by the Charter to the Eaft-India Company, from thofe which were granted by their own—that their own powers relate in general, only to objects of convenience or regulation, within the little diftrict of a clofe circumfcription, that the community at large never

can

can be deeply affected by any poffible exercife or abufe of thofe powers, and confequently that no neceffity can in the nature of things exift, wherefore their contract fhould be broken, and their charter refumed; whereas that the powers of the Eaft-India Company were imperial, their authority extended over vaft kingdoms, millions of people were happy or miferable in proportion to the good or the ill exercife of thefe powers; and that of the horrors of their government of their wars unjuftly undertaken, of their violence of their rapine, of their infatiable avarice, of their treacherous policy; there was not only no doubt, but an univerfal admiffion—I fay if they had compared all thefe effects with the worft that could poffibly flow from their own charters, they would have found that there was not only no refemblance between them, but that the fame juftice which had refumed the Company's, would have protected theirs.

Having conducted my reader to the diffolution of the parliament in 1784, and to the complete eftablifhment of the adminiftration of Mr. Pitt, by a decided majority in the new one; having endeavoured to account for the

the very extraordinary events which have been the subject of these few pages, from causes or motives that appear to me at least to be probable ones; having censured what I thought was deserving of animadversion, nor withheld my praise where I thought that praise could honestly be bestowed, and having judged in both cases with the freedom of history, and sustained my judgment by facts and by reasoning, not imposed it by insolent and dogmatical assertion; it may not be improper at this stage of my undertaking, and before I continue my sketch with the events which happened subsequently to the meeting of the new parliament, to enquire a little into the nature of this principle of resuscitation, which, as the author of the Sketch has observed, " has raised England from her de-
" pression, and has enabled her, unlike the
" other surrounding monarchies, to profit of
" her very misfortunes."

If the case, that a nation should flourish in a time of profound peace, that her commerce should extend, her navigation increase, and that every symptom of prosperity should appear in an accumulating and redundant capital—

pital—were entirely new, so that the like had never happened before; we might with justice ascribe such a very extraordinary event to very extraordinary means: we might, overlooking the industry and the spirit of an illustrious people, and the security which a system of administration of justice peculiarly excellent proposes, to property and acquisition of every kind; quite disregarding the advantages that a beneficent nature has lavished upon this favoured island, its situation, its climate, its means of support to its inhabitants, whom both land and sea conspire to bless with every production; and in short, setting at nought all moral and physical causes—I say, we might search for this vivifying spirit, not in their plain insufficiency, but in the powerful efficacy of a minister, " who, to incorruptible " integrity and unblemished manners, unites " strength of mind, severe œconomy, vigi- " lance which never sleeps, eloquence to " captivate, and vigour to subdue."

But, for my part, though I am willing to pay every tribute of admiration to this rare combination of endowments wherever I am convinced of its existence; I should be extremely

tremely loth to degrade the nation, which it is my pride that I belong to, or the national character, so far as to suppose for a moment, much less to assert, that this one man can operate the wonders, though he ingenuously admits some trifling co-operation from other causes, which the author of the Sketch so lavishes ascribes to the object of his superstitious reverence. For though in despotic governments (and I do assure that author that the British constitution whatever he may think, is not despotic), the sovereign power of one man has sometimes dispensed happiness over the land, and the ravages of despotism have yielded for a short interval to the godlike influence of virtuous sway, yet a country that is governed by laws, that boasts, and will maintain its liberty, is superior to the vicissitudes of particular characters : the prosperity of such a country is the effect of a constant cause; to say that it is the effect of the perishing nature of any individual, whether he be a minister or a king, is to libel the government, the laws, the character, the spirit of the people, and to substitute a cruel uncertainty to a certain expectation.

If there were no other proof of the operation of this constant cause, we should find it in the very enormous burthens which this nation has progressively endured for a century back, and ever since the practise of funding began. For though very little of the public debt has ever been discharged in the intervals of peace, and the nation has been much distressed at the conclusion of every war, yet we find it has always been able to engage in a new one with a renovated vigour, and to incur a fresh debt in addition to its former, to an amount that it never could have reached, nor approached, if it had attempted it, in the prosecution of the former. Now such an effect could only arise from the progressive state of prosperity, which the nation has been certain to enjoy in every interval of peace, by which capital has accumulated, and a vast auxiliary fund of property, of industry, and of consumption, which is the parent of taxes, has been acquired to supply the continually recurring exigencies of the state, and to furnish a new public estate to mortgage to new creditors whenever the occasion demanded it.

The

The case then of great national prosperity in a time of peace, is nothing new; and the author of the Sketch might have been satisfied with the good old causes, which, in a similar circumstance, have always produced the same effect; if the dazzling sun which irradiates the hemisphere, and vivifies our political nature, had not blinded his weak sight, or filled it in such a manner, as to exclude every other object.

But in the national depression, during the calamitous war that the nation sustained, we should find a particular cause, independantly of the general ones, which are always sure to assert themselves in real effects, upon such a change of circumstances, as from war to peace; wherefore the *apparent* prosperity of the country should strike us with admiration and delight: the mind of man is most sensibly affected by *contrast*; it is not the gradual progress of good that strikes the imagination, it is change from evil to good; and the good increases in value, not in respect of its intrinsic worth, but in respect of its vicinity to evil. Any effects that could flow from peace after a calamitous war, though *reason* should pronounce them inadequate to such a cause, would be received with gratitude by *sense*; and the bare absence of evil would be considered as the presence of good. In the case of former wars, though the conclusion of peace relieved the public from accumulating burthens; yet victory and conquest still flattered the vanity of Englishmen, and the change from war to peace, was a change from one species of good, not indeed rightly understood, to another species of good; and the evil being not known, or far removed, was lost in ignorance, or diminished by distance, so that the good was not exalted by the contrast; but when the nation, in a little time after the conclusion of the last peace, had recovered its tone, and all the debt was funded; when the redundant capital of the wealthy, instead of being consumed every year in the prosecution of a war, equally disgraceful and ruinous; instead of leaving no memory of itself behind, except in the accumulation of taxes and the oppression of industry, was obliged to pursue another course, and to fructify upon land, upon industry, upon private credit, and upon public securities; who was not struck

with

with this new state of things? Who did not enhance the good that was enjoyed from the consideration of the neighbouring evil? But this new state of things was necessary; it was the effect of no public regulation, of no political interference, which generally injures more than it does good: where capital accumulates in a country, and that country is in a desperate condition, where it does not, the price of every species of capital must increase from an increased number of purchasers, who lay out their annual surplus in the purchase of more stock. The prosperity of a country is the effect of this state of things, which must be found there; when it is not, it cannot be created without the perseverance of ages and a revolution in manners and in policy: to say that it is the sudden effect, or that it is in anywise contributed to by the powers of any one individual, is to sacrifice truth to servile adulation; it is to say that he is present in every man's bosom, that he animates his industry, that he is a party to his gains, that he inspires with enterprize, informs with prudence, and, by a particular interposition in every man's private conduct, creates a
general

general public effect, which can only be the result of the private conduct of all the individuals in the State.

But if we would enquire into the cause of national prosperity, which is nothing more than the sum of private success; I speak of the moral cause (for physical causes are doubtless possessed of a great power of co-operation), we shall discover it not in one man—not in a minister—not in a king—we shall discover it in twelve men, and in twelve men of no great seeming importance, who challenge no illustrious descent, nor appear with a splendour commensurate with their salutary and powerful efficacy; but who, generally speaking, improve their own property by an industrious application to trade or business, while they secure the property of others, by delivering, whenever it is litigated, impartial judgments from a jury-box.

It is the security of honest acquisition, from the oppression of power or the injustice of corruption, that vainly wanders in quest of an object to fasten upon in the floating and uncertain judicature; which has ever occasioned, by a certain operation, the prosperity of of Great Britain to be progressive; and unless industry is cramped by new impositions, and the State, by taking too large a proportion of the substance of the citizens, should crush activity by despair, instead of suffering it to be excited by generous hope, a constant effect will be the never-failing result of a constant cause. Whatever doubts may be entertained by many very thinking men concerning the reality of political liberty, in the actual state of the British constitution, and in the *practice* of the government; of the reality of civil liberty, while juries maintain their rights, no doubt can be entertained: and as the individual is not, in general, grossly affected by the measures of government (I except indeed the case of the extension of the excise), in the complete enjoyment of civil liberty he enjoys a state which is commensurate with his views and objects in life, which is sufficient to stimulate industry, and to awaken enterprize, by a certainty of the undisturbed possession of the fruits of his success, and to make him contributory, by his private gains and advantages, to the sum of public prosperity, which, as I have observed before,

and

and the observation cannot be too often repeated, is the result or agregate of private prosperity.

But before I dismiss this subject, there is a question that strikes me as not being unworthy of some discussion, viz. how far the advanced price of public securities is a criterion of national prosperity. The cause of this advanced price is very well known to originate in the increased competition of purchasers, for there being more buyers than sellers, which is always the case in the time of peace, when no new stock is brought to market to defray the excess of expence arising from an extraordinary emergency, it is plain that the commodity must keep rising in value, an effect that is merely produced by this circumstance, and is totally independant of any minister or administration, though this too is absurdly ascribed to a minister by fond panegyrick; and I am the more disposed to hazard an opinion upon this matter, because it is of service to the community, that it should not draw any very extravagant conclusions concerning its prosperity, great as I admit that it is, from a fact which is generally supposed to be the best criterion, and thus

thus by overrating its resources find itself disappointed in their amount, when it stands most in need of them from its wild engagements in schemes of continental politics and ridiculous chimeras, about a balance of power which cannot now affect us, whatever it might have done in the time of the usurpations of France.

Now the nature of a public debt is to accumulate property in the hands of some individuals at the expence of the whole community, and its effect is to multiply capitals, and to encrease the value of every kind of stock, by bringing to market a greater number of purchasers for that stock. We will suppose for a moment that all that capital which has accumulated in the hands of the public creditors, who lent the whole of the money for the carrying on the last war, was totally annihilated and extinguished, and that those taxes which are now paid to defray the interest of that vast debt were also to be annihilated; the probable consequence of such a state of things is, that there would be a less annual surplus over and above the expences of individuals, to constitute an annually accumulating capital, to go to market with to purchafe ftock. For the money that each perfon pays in taxes, to make up his proportion of the intereft of this hundred millions, or whatever it may be, being paid diftributively by the country at large, and falling in its great bulk upon the lower claffes of people, who are the great confumers in the nation; if their taxes were annihilated, it is probable that each perfon would live somewhat better than he did before, for the money faved by each by this means would be fo trifling as not to form any object worth laying by; befides that the poorer fort of people who fubfift by labour, and whofe agregate confumption is the great fund for taxation, though each may pay but a little, feldom do lay by any thing, if they can make both ends meet, as they fay, it being all that their fituation requires, or their prudence affects; and labour being the hereditary eftate which they receive, and wh ch they tranfmit, they are carelefs of every other fund, than that which nature has given them, and will preferve for their pofterity. But if we reinftate the debt and reftore the taxes, what is the confequence then? The taxes drawn from the whole body of the

people

people would find their way into the hands of a limited number of opulent perfons. The intereft thus paid every year, forming a very confiderable object to fuch limited number, though it is nothing difperfed throughout the whole mafs of the people, would probably accumulate every year, and form a frefh capital: but this capital muft be employed, and it muft therefore go to market to purchafe ftock of fome kind or other, which would continually rife in its price, by this continually encreafing competition.

And this effect would be perceived in its greateft force, prefently after the conclufion of a war, while the perfons were yet living who had advanced the whole money for carrying it on, for the great maffes of wealth remaining unbroken in their hands, would afford the greateft means of annual accumulations; though in time, when, from the neceffity of nature, a diftribution fhould take place, perhaps among large families, and the overplus of income would be reduced to the new poffeffors by the divifion, the effect would be much diminifhed; nor would the fame fymptom of profperity appear in redundant capitals,

tals, though no one could say, that the nation was at all the poorer. I do not know how I can illustrate my proposition relatively to this matter, better than by supposing, that the whole of the public debt of this kingdom was the property of one man. He surely would be able to spend a very small comparative part of it: all the rest, to the amount of eight or nine millions a year, would be an accumulating capital for him to go to market with, to purchase some employment for it. In such a state of things, does not the imagination revolt at the price that he would give for land, and for every other species of employment of capital, rather than suffer it to lie idle and useless in his coffers? if we break this mass of property into as many parts as there are public creditors in the kingdom, it is very certain that the accumulation would be less; for twenty-nine thousand people, after paying their expences, would have a less surplus to carry to market, than one single man would; and again, if we were to divide these parts into as many others, as there are people in the kingdom, the surplus of eight millions of people, after paying all

all their expences, would be lefs to go to market with than the furplus of twenty-nine thoufand; and though all would live better, the annual accumulation of capital would be much reduced; probably it would be none at all; but a general eafe and affluence would be the confequence, and furely the nation would not be at all the poorer from being quite out of debt. Again, if we fuppofe, that the inftead of nine millions to public creditors, the nation paid eighteen millions, we might reafonably infer, that the accumulations made by public creditors would, in that cafe, be the double of what they are now; and though the greater quantity of ftock that would be at market in that cafe would fomething relieve the competition of purchafers, yet it would not equalize it; and it is probable, that the price of every employment of capital would be extremely enhanced: but nobody that is in his fenfes would deny, but the nation would then be in a much worfe fituation than it is in now: and yet the generally acknowledged fymptoms of profperity would be greater, for the price of every employment of capital would be higher. From thefe reafonings
I con-

I conclude, that the price of the public funds is not a criterion of public profperity, but might be the effect of a ftate of things that would demand a conclufion directly oppofite to that which is ufually admitted.

I have engaged more deeply in thefe obfervations than a Sketch, which profeffes to be hiftorical, and to be converfant with facts, and not with fpeculative reafonings, can ftrictly be juftified in doing: but I fhall receive the indulgence of my reader, when he confiders the different nature of a hiftory which is contemporary with the facts it relates, from that which is converfant with facts, whofe confequences are now obliterated, and of which a complete example has been propofed by a cataftrophe of other facts; fo that in that cafe, nothing is left to fpeculation, but every thing is proved by experience. In our cafe, the CATASTROPHE has not yet arrived: the chain is ftill continuous; what the future links may be, depends upon the prudence of the prefent moment; nothing is proved by experience, but every thing is open to fpeculation; and to reafon, more than to relate, is the proper province of fuch a hiftory.

Another

Another real motive for entering pretty much at large into thefe matters, was to diffipate, if I could by any means fucceed, the errors that prevail fo much in men's minds, concerning the caufes of public profperity. That the nation is profperous (though I am compelled to fay much lefs fo than is concluded from the criterion that is generally reforted to) I do moft firmly believe, and I do moft fincerely rejoice. But the caufe of this is in the people, and in the laws; it is a permanent caufe; it is not, and it never has been, in a minifter. The beft that a minifter can do for the people, is to LEAVE THEM TO THEMSELVES, and his greateft poffible merit is a negative one. I do not fay but ufeful laws may be paft which, by their general tendency and operation, may have a *remote* effect, for they can have no other, upon the induftry of the people; but this I will fay, that fuch an effect never can be produced by the introduction of excifemen into the fhops, the cellars, the warehoufes of any clafs of citizens, ftill lefs can it be produced by keeping the country in a continual ferment, and exhaufting it by armaments upon every little trivial

trivial dispute; nor yet will a standing army, when the total alteration of the government of France has removed not only every cause of alarm, but even of jealousy from the only quarter where it could be entertained, and has rendered any army at all, for ought I can see, except what is sufficient to contend with the Sussex smugglers, quite unnecessary; be the best means of promoting the commerce, the industry, and the manufactures of the country. I say that a standing army *will* not be the best means of promoting these beneficial objects, because a minister ought not to be censured for not doing, what he has had scarcely time to do, for doubtless he will gladly seize the earliest opportunity of conforming to a conjuncture by which the people will be eased of such a heavy burthen, and the French revolution being now completely established, there can be no room for any longer delay; so that even this session may announce, or ought to do it, what his intentions are relatively to this measure, that the people expects, and the country, from a total change of circumstances, has a right to demand.

END OF PART THE FIRST.

www.ingramcontent.com/pod-product-compliance
Lightning Source LLC
Chambersburg PA
CBHW030016240426
43672CB00007B/979